Conversation Skills
How To Easily Talk To Anyone

Emma Watkins

Copyright © Emma Watkins Publishing

All rights reserved.

No part of this publication may be reproduced, distributed, or transmitted in any form or by any means, including photocopying, recording, or other electronic or mechanical methods, without the prior written permission of the publisher, except in the case of brief quotations embodied in critical reviews and certain other non-commercial uses permitted by copyright law.

Table of Contents

Let's Learn How To Talk To Anyone

Getting The Most Out of This Book...and your life!

Part One – You CAN Change!

This Changes Everything

Listening and Responding

Active Listening

Reading The Speaker

The New Connections

How To Properly Use Eye Contact, Even If You Are Shy

Overcoming The Real Problem

Actions vs. Words

The Key To Changing Your Social Skills

Reading Other People and How To Easily Respond To Them

Reading Different Types of People

Movements in Daily Life

Moving On

Part Two – You vs. Work

Dealing With Job Interviews

How To Easily Answer Questions

Talking About Yourself

Flipping The Script

Making Friends At Home and At Work

Navigating Close and Not Close Friends

Dealing With Parties!

How To Be Assertive

Speaking Out Loud: Small Talk to Public Speaking

Assertiveness Is A Valuable Tool

Part Three – Conversation Skills For Everyday Life

Tips For Dealing With Other People

Overcoming Fear

A Quick Exercise!
Things To Remember
How To Handle Formal Occasions
Event Rituals
Dealing With A Dinner Party
Moving On With Life

Let's Learn How To Talk To Anyone

"Communication – the human connection – is the key to personal and career success."
Paul J. Meyer

Having a conversation is one of the most basic human processes, yet at the same time communication is one of those things that we seem to take for granted. We teach people how to write and how to construct a sentence on paper, but there is little to no focus on the spoken word. In grade school, you are asked to make a few speeches, but that is often the end of it. Conversation is rarely formally taught. We are all expected to pick it up all on our own, with no help or guidance. Therefore it really is no wonder that some of us go off the path and find it difficult to have a flowing positive conversation.

This can be especially the case if you are an introverted person. For many years introversion was frowned upon. It was seen as a negative thing. Times have certainly changed. More and more, introverted people are being *celebrated*. You do not have to be the loudest in the room. You do not have to be the wittiest, charming, hilarious and interesting person in life to get ahead – although if this is what you want, then this book can definitely help you.

What I should make clear from the offset is that being a more introverted person should not mean you can not hold conversations, speak in public, make small chat with strangers or generally be a fun and interesting person to be around. Being this sort of person is very possible, with the advice I will give you in this book.

The lack of proper conversation education seems utterly insane when you think about the importance that your ability to communicate will have on the rest of your life. Not everyone needs to know the value of pi to be successful in life, but we all need to know how to talk to other people to achieve our goals. We all need to know how to connect with other people if we are going to live happy, complete lives. This is where this book comes in. To fill in the gaps you may have missed or to put you back on the path to easy flowing positive conversations and interactions with people.

Humans are social creatures, but that doesn't mean that these things come to us naturally. I am someone who has struggled with shyness in the past. It held me back for a long time. I know how it feels. With the knowledge, advice, and skills I am going to pass on with this book, I was able to overcome my issues. However, even today as someone who regularly speaks at public events, I still sometimes have slight wobbles where I revert to my former shy self for a few seconds.

Occasionally when entering a social situation, I can still feel the butterflies start to lightly flutter inside my stomach and I momentarily look down at the ground. This feeling now passes pretty quickly, but I am just telling you this to show you that you are not alone. I have been in the same situation you may find yourself in today. I am here to tell you that you *can* get better. If anyone had told me a few years ago that one day I would be speaking in front of hundreds of people at public events and then wandering around aftershow events, easily chatting with complete strangers…well, I would have thought you were mad!

My mother calls me a late bloomer. That is something I have heard quite a bit. I have been told that I didn't go about life in the right way, and a lot of that had to do with letting my healthy introversion turn into unhealthy shyness. Right after high school, I was so nervous about making the wrong move and embarrassing myself that I often didn't do *anything*. Sometimes it is just easier to hide from the world or anything that scares or challenges us. There is a certain safety and a certain comfort in just doing nothing. The problem is, doing nothing does not offer a fulfilled or happy life.

My late teens were difficult. I was worried about moving away from home and living in a dorm. I was fretting because all of my friends were leaving and I was going to be on my own. I had made three good friends in grade one and those were the people that I was still hanging out with in high school. I was worried that I would never make any more friends. I found chatting with people awkward. I never quite knew what to say. Conversations felt stunted.

I was letting fear get the better of me. That's when I decided that I wanted, or to be more accurate that I *needed* to do something about the fear that was starting to take over my life. By purchasing this book, I am guessing this is a point that you may have reached as well. Perhaps you, as I did in my past, decided enough was enough. Does any of the following sound familiar to you?

- I wanted to be better at talking to people.
- I wanted to know what other people knew that seemed to make it so easy for them.
- At times I was afraid of being myself with people. I was afraid of appearing foolish, and I was afraid of being laughed at. (Don't ever let anyone tell you these are not real fears. They are. I have felt them. I know them well.)
- I wanted life to be a little easier. Smoother. Less stressful.
- I wanted to enjoy social events.
- I wanted to make more friends, more successful romantic connections and better career links.

If any of that seems familiar to you, then you have already done the important thing - by buying this book you have committed to actually doing something about it.

I needed to change things in my life and change things I most definitely did. I will discuss this in detail throughout this book, but here is the most basic story, to serve as an introduction to myself.

To improve my social encounters and therefore improve my life, I knew I needed to take action. After following some of the advice I have laid out in this book, I then went out and the first thing that I did was take a job in sales, a role I *never* thought I would be able to do in the past. I knew I had to get over my social fear right away, because my only job was to talk to people! If I wasn't talking to people then I wasn't making any money. Sales is a little different than working in retail, or customer service, because the emphasis is on building a relationship. It is not just knowing the products; it is about knowing people and knowing how to talk to them beyond just trying to sell them the latest gadget. Through research and my own methodology, I devised my own plan to help me deal with my lack of communication skills and social anxiety as fast and successfully as possible.

The next step for me was to enroll in University. My first degree was in History, and then I moved on to Psychology. I loved the social sciences; humans, and societies are fascinating to me. I wanted to understand how we all fit together and how we worked and lived together. This is an area I continue to research and work in to this very day.

I think the reason I found it so fascinating was because I always used to feel like an alien sent to Earth to discover their customs and traditions. I watched others, even members of my own family, and they just seemed to *know* how to fit in. I was sidelined and unsure of how to participate in the social practices that I witnessed all around me. I wasn't a mute, but I did find conversation troublesome. It never seemed to flow. Social engagements were difficult for me.

During this time I had managed, using much of the advice in later chapters of this book, to find and marry the most wonderful man. He knew my natural introversion would sometimes lead into unnatural and harmful social anxiety and I think he saw me as a bit of a project. Over the past few years, we have really helped each other in many ways as we both developed and grew in life. He has been a driving force in my life and without him I don't know if I would have had the courage to undertake this transformation, start this career and ultimately write this book. Do remember that this is coming from the woman who once struggled to even make eye contact with the opposite sex, let alone hold a proper interesting conversation!

I know that many people are not as lucky as I am, and they will not have someone there to push them forward. This is why I wrote this book. I sincerely hope it can help you to have more meaningful and successful conversations and connections with people and ultimately to bring more happiness to your life.

In writing this book, I had a very simple goal in mind. My aim is to teach you the art of conversation. And it really is an **art**. While some people are naturally talented artists, many others learn the craft through education.

I have broken up this book into different parts in order to cover the mechanics of conversation, easy tools to immediately improve your communication skills, methods to overcome real-life scenarios and skills for better personal interaction, even for the shy person.

The book is going to examine social situations and provide you with practical advice for overcoming the obstacles that are holding you back from having meaningful conversations. It will also provide you with exercises, tips, and tricks to make you a more confident speaker and a more engaged listener.

Easily Be Better Around People

Who is this book for? Quite simply, this book is for anyone, young or old, male or female who feel like they might need assistance in communicating with people, for whatever reason.

Many people feel that they need help with conversation. They need to know what to say and just as importantly, *how* to say it. They want better results from their interactions and conversations with people. Maybe their shyness is holding them back, or perhaps they just feel they are a little awkward during conversations and don't quite know what to say. Shyness affects us all differently. For some people it is a mild irritant while for others, it causes great distress that can even lead to depression if not addressed. Shyness is something that had affected me in the past, so I know *exactly* how it feels. Thankfully I have made mammoth strides over the last fifteen years and gotten to a place where I feel safe. I can honestly say that I am no longer letting fear rule my life and my hope is I can help you feel the same way.

My life is very different these days. I make speeches all over the world. I have taught classes and hosted corporate retreats. These are things that I would never have thought possible fifteen, or even ten years ago. I keep pushing myself to do more and to keep growing. I want to encourage you to do the same thing. It is easier than you think. Really!

This book is also for people who just want to learn more about conversations. You may not feel like you are very shy at all. Maybe you reach out to people all the time, but you feel like you're not having meaningful conversations. You are talking, but you are not building relationships. This book is definitely for you. A conversation is more than just two people talking. There is an art to it.

This book is a journey, written over the course of the last fifteen years. The research for it started long before I even knew I was writing a book! I want to take you along on this journey, but you have to be ready. Just like any other program, this will only work if you put in the work and have a strong desire to be a better communicator in life. If you do, then I guarantee this book will help you as it has for many thousands before you. Let us begin!

Getting The Most Out Of This Book…and your Life!

"The best way to predict the future is to create it."
Abraham Lincoln

Cons. They are everywhere. Books and programs that promise you can lose weight in 48 hours, learn a new language in 5 days, only work 2 hours a week but be a millionaire and so on and so on. Learning new communication skills is not easy, but also it does not have to be difficult. It just involves a little bit of work and dedication. Anyone that claims you can do this stuff overnight without any work is quite frankly trying to con you – I await the lawyers to contact me about that sentence, but I felt it needed to be said!

This book is trying to help you, and so am I, but the most important thing really is *you*. The very fact that you have bought this book shows me that you are serious about this matter and that you are willing to put the work in. I have exercises and activities for you…do not groan, I know, I know, nobody likes exercises, but trust me, there aren't many and they really do work! The exercises will give you solid and practical ways for you to apply the skills you learn. It is entirely up to you, but I promise that if you actually do them, you will gain so much more from this book.

My advice to you would be to start by getting a notebook. If you prefer to go digital, then this is fine. Whatever works best for you. Throughout the book, I am going to offer you **Journaling Cues**. Each one of these cues will allow you the opportunity to explore your feelings about the topic of each chapter. It has been proven time and time again that writing things down helps you understand them better and most importantly helps you remember them. When you are entering a conversation, especially with someone you don't really know, it is very easy to forget everything you have learned. Writing things out helps the advice to become imprinted in your brain. It helps it all to become second nature, allowing the conversation to flow easier.

Journaling Cue: What are you hoping to get out of this book?

Take a few minutes and list the goals that you had in mind when you first decided to buy this book. Think about what it is that you want to accomplish personally, or professionally through better communication skills. Drill down a level and try to write as much detail as possible.

So we just had our first Journaling cue. It wasn't that hard, right? I firmly believe that writing down your feelings is a good way to sort through the clutter in your mind. It is not just me who believes this; the benefits of journaling are documented time and time again. The amount of successful business people and world leaders who do this is quite staggering. During my own personal journey, I used journals as a way to document my progress, and many of the stories that you will hear in this book were written down in one of the seven notebooks I filled.

Writing things down, taking that extra step, is going to help you process the daily interactions that you have with people as you practice your new conversation skills. It is how you're going to get the most out of this experience. So don't stop at the journaling cues I leave you. Try to find the time to write down your thoughts and feelings at every stage of this journey. I take fifteen minutes to a half hour, at the end of every day, to go through my daily interactions and write down my experiences. That's right; I still do it to this day as I continue to find it hugely beneficial.

While I enjoy it, it is also not necessarily something that I need to do anymore. I now feel very comfortable talking to people. On rare occasions, I get a little anxiety or stumble on my words, but this is totally natural. **Everyone** does it at times. The truth is these things never completely go away, but they are incredibly manageable now and barely affect my life at all. I still write in my journals because it is helpful to process my daily interactions. You may get to a point where you won't need to write in your journal, but I personally feel it is very beneficial when starting out in this process.

You don't necessarily have to spend hours reading over and analyzing what you have written. Most people don't. It's the process of writing or typing out your feelings out that actually makes the difference.

The important thing is that you take the time for *you.* To improve your life, you must first understand your life better. I have put everything I have into the book, but at the end of the day, all I can do is tell you what has helped me and the many people I have taught over the years and hope it helps you too.

Part One – You CAN Change!

We will start with you, your physical self. You are the one standing there next to the other person. You are the person who is engaged in the conversation. You are the person always present in your own social encounters. You are quite important in this situation ;)

If you want to understand the importance of you in a conversation, you need only to think about how you analyze the people you're talking to. As they walk up to you immediately notice their hair, their clothes, the way they are standing or carrying themselves and in general how they are looking. From the moment you notice a person and realize that you are possibly about to engage in a conversation, you start to analyze them. Everyone does it. It is inbuilt in our brains; we have very little control over this.

It is an unconscious action for you, and it's the same type of process for the other person. You are both standing there analyzing each other. When it comes to the all-important first impressions, your body language, clothing, style and general posture may have more weight than even the words you are choosing to use.

I am not advocating three-piece suits or trips to the salon before every conversation in order to try and impress people. I am just saying that all of these things could have an impact on the quality of the conversation, perhaps even more so than you are currently aware. One of the first things they tell you in sales is that you are not selling a product; you are selling yourself. This is also true of engaging in conversation, especially with somebody new. You need to present yourself in a way that makes other people actually want to talk to you. Unfortunately, the job of your physical appearance does not end there.

So this section is about the mechanics of a conversation. Your body and your eyes are huge parts of this, but we are going to start with your ears. In my opinion, the ears are *the* most important physical component of any successful and happy conversation. Ears allow us to listen to the other person. Successful and flowing conversation is more about listening than it is about talking.

This Changes Everything

"Listening is a positive act; you have to put yourself out to do it."
David Hockney

Listening is the most important job you have in a conversation. Anyone can talk, but it is very difficult to truly listen to someone. It's not something that comes naturally to many people. In fact, many people go through life just waiting for their turn to talk. They sit and nod, half listening to the other person before interrupting with something that totally ruins the flow of the conversation. And then the other person does the same thing. And so it continues on and on.

This is not a conversation; it is simply two people talking **at** each other. This is unhealthy and unproductive. This is what you might have been doing all of your life. Why do people do this? There are many possible reasons, but one might be simply that you are afraid because you don't know how to respond effectively. At times some people shy away from actual human contact whenever possible. If this sounds like you then you have been experiencing stunted talking instead of conversation. In this chapter, we are going to learn about how to change this bad habit. We are going to learn about the delicate art of listening.

I will talk about this in much more detail later in the book, but eye contact is a very important part of listening. It is more important to look the person in the eyes when you are the one listening than when you are the one doing the talking.

When the other person is in the act of talking, it is your job to show that you are interested in what they are saying. Eye contact is a vital part of that. It says that you are focused on the other person and the conversation. It says you are interested in what they are saying. It says you want to be here, in this moment. Most importantly, it shows respect for the other person.

"Well, I am really good at multi-tasking! I can listen to someone and text at the same time!" you might say.

No. No, you cannot. You think you can, but really, you cannot. And this is not just an opinion. It is fact. Test after test has shown it is impossible to *truly* engage with someone (and for the other person to feel respected) if you are doing something at the same time such as texting on your phone. Not only is it your job to show that you're interested and engaged, it is also incredibly rude to be involved in other activities while you are supposed to be listening. People, shy or not, can tell when they are being ignored. **And nobody likes to be ignored.**

Generally speaking, people don't just come out and say that they don't want to talk to you. Talking is only one of several ways of communicating. Texting, or even just holding the phone in your hand is a great way to communicate that you would rather be doing something else than be present in the moment with the other person.

Many people like to do something such as play with a mobile phone as some sort of safety blanket or as a defense mechanism. Once upon a time, this was me. I rarely had my phone out of my hand when I was in any sort of social situation. You hold the phone in your hand to make people think that you're busy. It's because you're shy or you feel awkward, and we both know that, but it is telling the others around you that you are not interested in a conversation. Cell phones and other defensive mechanisms make us feel safe, but ultimately they are nearly always a negative thing. They may be wrapping a protective barrier around us, but at the same time, they prevent us from making meaningful connections and having flowing conversations.

After one rather embarrassing party where I felt everything I said was awkward and out of time, a close friend advised me to put my phone away at the next social event. For the longest time, I had no idea where to put my hands. It was something that really bothered me. So I put them in my pockets, or I folded my arms across my chest, both of which were obviously mistakes. Even the most basic body language skills book will tell you that this is the wrong technique to apply. It is defensive and tells the other person that you would rather be alone.

You may ask how this relates to listening? It is simple. One of the biggest (and sometimes most difficult) parts of listening is convincing others that you *are* actually listening. To stay engaged in a conversation, a person needs to feel like the other person is listening to them and is interested in what they have to say.

<u>Journaling Cue:</u> Are you a good listener?

Many of us think we are listening whenever we hear a person's voice. The fact is if you are just waiting for your turn to talk then you are not listening. Think about how many times you have actually listened to someone.

How often do you leave a conversation not really knowing what the other person was really talking about?
Do you feel these exchanges were positive, productive, successful and enjoyable?
Or do you feel they were missing something?

Try to be completely honest.

Listening and Responding

"We listen to people at a rate of 125-250 words per minute, but think at 1,000-3,000 words per minute."
Kristin Piombino

Hearing is something that just happens. A lot of the time it is not something that you are doing, it is something that happens to you. If you are only hearing a conversation, then you are not really having one. Hearing a conversation is very different from *engaging* in a conversation.

Distractions, such as a mobile phone, take away from our ability to interact with people on a human level. I don't mean to drum on about phones so much, but in this day and age, they are proving to be a huge barrier between people in real life. When we try to divide our attention between conversation and phone calls, apps, and other electronic chaos, we lose an opportunity to make a real connection. These connections are an important part of the human experience, and they are worth more of our time than all of our devices combined.

Let me say that there is no doubt that digital devices are incredible. I absolutely adore mine. These incredible inventions allow us the opportunity to meet people we might never have met. They give us a world of information at our fingertips. However, study after study is showing that the rapid growth of smart phones, especially with younger and younger children, is negatively affecting our actual real-life communication skills. All the apps allowing us to connect with people online are absolutely useless if we cannot then communicate with them effectively offline!

As smartphones become even more ingrained in our culture, this trend is sure to increase. Kids today seem to be born attached to electronic devices. Give any toddler an iPad and just see what they can do. It is quite amazing. Perhaps it is about time we realized that sometimes we just need to unplug for a little while.

For many people I have talked to, the smartphone is their go-to safety device. They have told me stories such as standing in a bar, even with friends, and feeling awkward as they didn't really know how to join in the conversation; therefore the phone comes out and thus throws them even further out of the communication circle. In doing this, you are missing opportunities for genuine human interaction and growth in life.

Listening involves taking an interest in what the speaker is saying. Looking at your phone or around the room is the easiest way to tell the person that you're not interested. You are putting up a wall and letting that person know that you do not really value their opinion. You are unconsciously saying that you are bored. You are saying that you do not want to be there.

This may be the first time you have truly thought about conversation as anything other than an everyday interaction. Let's take a minute to reframe it. Think of it is a *social contract*. A contract is full of rules and guidelines. The things I am telling you in this book are guidelines that the participants need to follow before they can properly engage in meaningful conversation. When you ignore the guidelines, then you are sending a direct insult to that person and devaluing them and what they are saying. The contract is broken.

During a conversation, there are many factors that can distract you, or make you appear distracted. There are a million little things that you can do that take away your focus and let the other person know that you're not listening. Fidgeting and unnecessary jerky movements are a sign to people that they are being ignored. Playing with your hair, scratching your neck, fumbling with your clothes are also all negative signals to the other person. It doesn't matter what you're doing. The general rule is if you are fidgeting, you're not listening. Obviously, I am not saying you need to stand completely still like a statue, but you do need to keep your fidgeting to a minimum, especially during a more serious or deep conversation.

As I said earlier in this book, I previously suffered from being quite shy and awkward in social situations. When conversations began to feel awkward and unsuccessful, doodling became my favorite form of fidgeting. Many people do this, and many people try to excuse it away. During my teaching career at University, I have heard all sorts of excuses for it. A young woman actually told me that she couldn't listen unless she was doodling. The pictures can be cute, and may add something to the aesthetic value of the finished notes, but they take away from the listener's ability to understand, retain, and comprehend the information.

"But I am a multitasker!" I hear you scream!

No, you aren't. This is a common misconception. There are some people who are *better* at multitasking than others, but **NOBODY** truly gives one hundred percent of themselves to anything while also trying to do something else. It is mathematically impossible, to say the least.

"A recent Harvard Business Review post said multitasking leads to as much as a 40% drop in productivity, increased stress, and a 10% drop in IQ."
Bergman, 2010

The main problem with distractions is that they tell the speaker that you're not interested in having a conversation with them. You look like you are too busy, or even worse, you look like you *feel* you are too important to give them your time. Many of these distractions stem from your own social awkwardness, and your lack of self-worth, but they send a very different message to the other person.

How do you get past these feelings? The first thing to do is to get out of yourself. By that I mean take an interest in the other person in the conversation. Focus your energy on them, and you will see that this pays off. If you take an interest, generally speaking, people will respond to that, and they will pay more attention to what you are saying as well.

To properly take an interest in the other person, and make them the speaker in the conversation, you need to employ a technique that has become a buzz word over the last several years; **"Active Listening."**

I know, everyone talks about it. The phrase is so ubiquitous it is almost meaningless, but how many people actually know what it really means? Here's a little rundown on the principles behind the buzzword and why it is so important.

Active Listening

At its most basic, Active Listening is simply taking an interest in what the other person is saying. As the listener, you are constantly sending verbal and non-verbal cues to the speaker that you're interested in what they have to say. You smile, you nod, and you (hopefully) engage in the dialogue. In active listening, it is also important to read the response of the speaker and act accordingly. Too much of any of those ingredients can be a problem; no one wants to talk to a bobble-head doll, nodding constantly!

The nodding and responding are just a select few of the factors in a much larger process. Active listening is a system that helps us understand and retain the information that we are receiving in a conversation. The fact is the average person cannot retain much of what they hear. A study conducted by *Frost & Rybolt* in 1983 concluded this; *"On average, viewers who just watched and listened to the evening news could only recall 17.2% of the content when not cued, and the cued group never exceeded 25%."*

The reasons behind these findings are pretty simple; it is because during the evening news we are passively listening. We are not engaging in a dialogue with the newsreader. Information is being tossed at us, and our brains are attempting to hold onto as much as they can. Which in reality is really not that much!

Engaging with the Dialogue

Properly engaging in dialogue is essential if we want to be successful in social situations. The question is how do we engage in active listening without annoying people? It is really easy to irritate the other person with this tactic if we do not do it correctly. Too many people think that active listening is automatically repeating everything that is being said to you. It is not. It is about processing what the other person has said and putting your own spin and view on it.

This processing also has the added benefit of helping to alleviate confusion. If you're trying to put things into your own words, you're going to find that the other person will correct you. Even though you are speaking the same language as the person that you are conversing with, the words don't always mean the same thing to different people. Let use the word *'couple'* as an example. It means different things to different people, and it means different things depending on what you're actually talking about. If you're talking about people, a couple refers to two people. If you mean drywall screws, a couple could be two, or it might be a handful. **Context is important when you're trying to achieve understanding.**

The key to active listening is that you are directly engaging with the other person's words. Whether it is repeating or paraphrasing, you are taking in everything that is being said and communicating to the other person that you are engaged in the conversation. Engage with the other person and ask questions. This is the 'active' part. You are taking action to ensure that you properly understand the conversation and you are showing the other person that you are interested in what they are saying.

Reading the Speaker

As previously stated, one of the keys to active listening it to properly focus on the speaker. You have to gauge everything you are doing by how the speaker is reacting to your active listening signals. It is great to agree with the speaker, but too much interjection on your part can throw a speaker off his game. You should make eye contact, but not too much, or eye contact that is too intense can be unsettling. Nodding is an appropriate active listening technique, but if you are nodding as the speaker describes a death in the family then you are sending out the wrong message altogether! You need to learn how to read the situation.

The main ingredient in active listening is **you**. You need to be engaged and focused. As my friends at *Skillsyouneed.com* explain:

"It is perfectly possible to learn and mimic non-verbal signs of active listening and not actually be listening at all. It is more difficult to mimic verbal signs of listening and comprehension."

I would add that it can be dangerous to only mimic the *signs* of active listening. When you engage in this practice, you are sending out clear social signals. If you are nodding along to hate speech or other rhetoric and not actually listening you may send the wrong message about yourself to the speaker and other people around you.

Reading the speaker involves carefully watching their signals. I will discuss this more in the section on body language, but you have to understand the signals the speaker is putting out.

How are they standing?
What is their head doing?
Where are they looking and for how long?

These are all important questions you should ask. The information you gleam from this will allow you to know the best path to next take in the conversation.

Comprehension

The dictionary definition of comprehension is *"the ability to understand something"*. Active listening, when done properly, should add to your comprehension of the speaker's topic. As you engage more with the dialogue, you will begin to understand more. The more you understand, the more you will be able to say in response, which leads to successful and flowing communication. If you are unsure about anything that is being said then just ask! Some people think it is rude to ask for clarification, but in reality, it is quite the opposite. Asking for clarification of key points is a good way to show that you are listening. On occasion I have asked for clarification even when I *did* understand what the other person was saying, simply to show them I am interested in what they have to say and want to know more.

The key to asking a clarification question is to ask an open-ended question. These questions allow the speaker to expand on their point and should provide a deeper understanding for the entire audience. I am going to provide an example here, but I first want to give you a situation. In the sample questions below the active listener is trying to gather more information about an incident in the office involving a man named Lenny and a man named Jeff.

Here's the first example:
"What happened at the office today?"
In this example, the listener is taking an interest in the person's life and has asked them a question that allows them plenty of space for elaboration. The only fault of the question is that it is not very specific. The listener may end up hearing about her co-worker's lunch, or the latest shipment of pens.

A more specific question would be:
"What happened today with Jeff and Lenny?"
The question has gotten more specific, and now the speaker knows exactly what incident the listener is asking about. The danger of getting specific can be seen in this next question.

Here's a negative example:
"Why was Lenny such a jerk today?"

This question is technically an open-ended question. It needs more than a yes or no answer from the speaker, but at the same time, it offers a judgment. The listener is leading the speaker. By letting the speaker know that he/she supports Jeff, the listener has changed the answer that the speaker was going to give. A good open-ended question should offer no judgment.

The New Connections

"When you learn something new, your brain grows new cells and builds new connections which has proven benefits for problem-solving and memory skills. Learning can help improve cognitive ability and memory function and can help ward off Alzheimer's disease and dementia."
Kimberley Fowler

This quote is from a blog about seniors, but it doesn't change the fact that it is beneficial to learn things, no matter what age you are. Practice your listening and grow some new brain cells at the same time. Seems like a good deal to me!

Do not underestimate the power of listening. In all my years of research, I would say this is the thing that many people who suffer with conversation skills do poorly. They do not realize the power of listening, learning and comprehending and how it can improve your own life as well as making the other person so much more receptive to you. It really is a win-win situation.

My favorite part of this chapter is that it starts us off with a very common theme that runs through the whole book; we don't think about everyday communications. Listening doesn't come naturally to everyone. Talking doesn't come naturally to everyone, but we all assume that communicating is a natural process that we should all understand. This book is going to continue to discuss the social interactions that you take for granted as natural and turn them on their heads so that you can understand them as social processes. Before we move on, here are some things to remember.

- Hearing is *not* just listening. It is so much more than that.

- Your job as the listener is to prove that you *are* actually listening.

- Multitasking is a myth! Do not believe it!

How To Properly Use Eye Contact, Even If You Are Shy

Eye contact is a difficult but important subject to cover. Despite what some people claim, there really are no hard and fast rules about duration, consistency, or frequency with which you should look at someone during a conversation. In many cases, you will be forced to rely on the other person's physical response to your eye contact to dictate what you should do next.

However, eye contact really is a subject that is becoming increasingly important to talk about for various reasons. One of these reasons is because of the number of people now working in remote locations, shopping online and generally spending less and less time with people in real life. We are spending less time dealing with people face to face. We talk to our employers or coworkers over the phone or email where we don't have to worry about eye contact.

I work from home and at times whenever I leave the house it can feel like a mole person coming out of his cave! I spend the first few minutes just trying to get over the bright lights and the loud noises! I have to be careful to ensure I get plenty of actual real-life human interaction every day. Working from home is an incredible gift, but it can have huge flaws if not dealt with correctly.

The slow decline in real life interactions are dulling our social skills, especially when it comes to eye contact. When we do have to speak to someone in real life or attend a social gathering, we are less trained at this sort of scenario than people 50 years ago. This is a serious problem for some people, and unfortunately, it is an issue that only seems to be getting worse.

Bad advice on eye contact is incredibly common. I don't want to name any names here, but some truly awful books have been released with embarrassing, and at times, dangerous advice.

One such book claims that people should envision a triangle on the face of the person that they are talking to. The top point of the triangle is supposed to be between the person's eyes with the other two sides going to the corners of their mouth. Your eyes are supposed to focus in the middle of this triangle and then move them around the triangle constantly even 3 seconds.

May I suggest, very strongly, that you do not **ever** do this! This is ridiculous advice and more likely to end with the police being called than having a successful conversation.

This is just an example of the millions of pieces of bad advice available about eye contact being thrown about these days. You would likely scare people less if you actually drew a triangle on their face, than if you sat around counting the number of seconds you spent staring at the corner of their mouth!

There are many people who try to quantify eye contact to study the subject scientifically. *Quantified Communications*, an analytics company based in Austin, Texas believes that we need 60-70% eye contact during a conversation to build a connection. They also assert that a good gaze lasts seven to ten seconds. This is not necessarily bad advice, but personally, I find studies like this a little too analytical. We are humans with dynamic emotions, forced into ever-changing situations with a huge variety of people. The more scientific advice is often hard to use in real life and can, in fact, cause more harm than good.

When it comes to academic subjects like history, or science, I find statistics are very helpful. However, they can be hard to apply to real-life situations. What I would advise you to take away from these numbers is the fact that during a conversation you should spend more time looking someone in the eye than not looking someone in the eye. That is good general advice and a lot easier to follow!

<u>Journaling Cue:</u> Are you afraid of eye contact? Do you know why? Be honest with yourself.

Another way to think of this question is what is it about eye contact that makes it so uncomfortable for many of us? What do you feel when you look into the eyes of your family, friends, co-workers, or your boss? Think about your struggles with eye contact. Can you identify a pattern?

Eye contact is all about the feeling. It is about being natural. This may seem like terrible news for people who feel like they are naturally awkward, but do not fret! Despite how it may seem now, you really can get past this block. You can learn how to establish and engage in meaningful and effective eye contact. Unfortunately, there is no standard formula for this, but there are plenty of little tricks that you can use to make eye contact seem natural and avoid the dreaded awkward stare!

The Easiest Way To Learn Effective Eye Contact…and what not to do!

The big question many of you may be asking is when does eye contact cross the line and turn into staring? The line at which a person's persistent eye contact becomes uncomfortable is different for everyone. Again no set rules should be followed for this but as general guidance to avoid crossing the line into staring I would suggest moving your head at least once every twenty seconds. It doesn't sound like much, but this is a theory that you can test out on your own. Using the stopwatch on your phone try looking at someone you know. I am talking full on direct eye contact, and see just how long it takes for both of you to feel uncomfortable. Now try it with a stranger *(…just kidding!)*.

So how do you move your head every twenty seconds and keep it natural? This can be as simple as changing the angle of your head or looking around the room. You do not need to overthink this too much. You also don't need to time this exactly! These are just rough guidelines! A good place to glance at is the speaker's hands. The other person will subconsciously pick up on this and consider you still very engaged in what they are saying, as the hands are often quite expressive during a conversation. The point of these exercises is to break up the eye contact while not appearing to be avoiding the other person or looking like you are bored. The difference between effective eye contact and staring can be quite stark. Effective eye contact says, *"I'm interested in what you're saying"*. This is a good thing. However, when it crosses the line into staring, for a lot of people this says *"I want to lock you in my basement."* Which is not really the look you want to go for at a party, right?

You have to find a way to avoid staring. So feel free to incorporate pieces of art and other focal points around the room into your line of sight. Give it a quick glance. Adjust your head slightly. This not only serves to maintain the conversation, but it provides a needed breaking of eye contact.

Another way to differentiate your eye contact from staring is to know your own face. An odd thing to say I know, but stay with me here! We have all heard people speak of *'resting cross face,'* – ok it is often called something else, but let's keep it clean and call it the resting cross face!

This is often something that is joked about, but in reality, many people do not realize that they do this and just how detrimental it can be. I have personally struggled with this for many years. If I'm not smiling, then people think that I am mad at them or they constantly ask what is wrong. It doesn't matter what the circumstances are socially, I have to be smiling or people get very upset with me!

The 'resting cross face' also increases the likely hood that people will take your eye contact as staring. You may be unaware of your own facial expressions, and this is where talking with a close friend and testing different faces can actually help. Just like all things, fixing resting cross face is all about moderation. Changing from a frown to a crazy looking smile as if you're auditioning to play the

Joker in Batman, is not going to make people more likely to talk to you. They will likely run away from you very fast! You have to find a relaxed, and natural looking smile which is where the next exercise comes in.

A Quick & Helpful Exercise

This exercise may seem very silly and even simplistic, but it really does work. It is amazing how little we know about our own faces. Knowing how a certain expression feels in our muscles will help you the next time you are in a social situation.

Step 1 – Get a mirror and place a seat in front of it or stand if you feel more comfortable.

Step 2 - While looking at yourself in the mirror, begin to practice making the different smiles that you do every day.

Step 3 - Find the smiles that work for your facial features. The ones that make you feel good about yourself. The smiles that look natural and not too forced or uncomfortable.

Step 4 - Hold these smiles until you can feel the muscles that are being used then slowly begin to relax your face. Repeat the exercise at least three times.

This may seem foolish, but it *will* help you to understand your face and how it works. You will obviously not have a mirror in front of you when you're engaged in conversation, therefore, you need to be sure you know what your face is doing. You need to know how it feels. For some people, this might feel like a very silly exercise but try to embrace it!

"Hold on!" I hear you cry, *"This chapter is about eye contact, not smiling!"*

Absolutely, you caught me, this exercise is all about smiling, but if you also look at your eyes in the mirror, you will see that your expression completely changes the tone of your eye contact. A smile makes your face look receptive to conversation. Immediately your eyes lighten, and you are not staring; you are looking. A smile can completely change the way people receive and interpret your eye contact, and that is something that you have to think about when entering a room or engaging in conversation.

Improving Your Self-Worth, Assertiveness and Social Skills

I've already briefly talked about this, but I felt like it needed its own section as it is very important. There is a direct and very real correlation between how you feel about yourself inside and how you respond to the people around you. People are always walking around comparing themselves based on the supposed social metrics of success, wealth, beauty, fitness, etc. At times it can be hard to stop this process and allow yourself to be happy with the person that you are right now in the moment. Many psychologists describe this process of comparison as your inner voice as Dr. Kristen Neff states:

"This internalized dialogue of critical thoughts or "inner voices" undermines our sense of self-worth and even leads to self-destructive or maladaptive behaviors, which make us feel even worse about ourselves."

This does not mean that we are hearing voices, but that we hear the criticism about ourselves that we have internalized from outside stimuli. Our parents, teachers, coaches, peers and mass media all contribute to building this inner voice over time.

I watch the Olympics religiously every four years. I watch the Olympians as they enter the opening ceremonies and I find myself saying things like, *"Can you believe how young she is?"* or, *"She is in amazing shape."* I find myself developing all sorts of jealous and insecure thoughts as I begin to compare myself to these athletes. Some of them have million dollar contracts. Some of them have good looks **and** skills that I will never have. They are the top athletes in the world. They are the absolute best of the best.

As I watch these events, I find that I have to remind myself that I am not an athlete. It doesn't matter if I can't throw a discus very far. It doesn't matter that I know I would face plant if I even tried to pole vault. I love what I do. I find it very rewarding. I have a beautiful family that loves me very much. It is good enough for me just to be the person that I am. I am not an Olympian. I am not an actor or a model. I am not a millionaire business owner. And that is perfectly ok.

These are important things to remember as you walk through life comparing yourself to other people. Unfortunately, it is practically impossible to shut off that voice. Your inner voice is a part of you. It will likely always be there. Sometimes it holds your hand and helps you. Sometimes it attacks you, at times quite viciously. However, you really don't have to let it rule your life. The more aware you become of the triggers which bring out your insecurities, the easier it is to quiet the voice by reassuring yourself that you have value.

I remember a job in sales I had many years ago, at a time in my life when I was awkward during conversations and more than a little shy about human communication. I went and bought a load of expensive tapes, all about becoming a better sales person. I was nervous about doing sales, and I was borderline frightened about talking to people. I needed help, and I needed it fast. I wanted to figure this new job out. Most of these tapes had a part where they told their listeners to get in front of a mirror each day and reaffirm your value. I thought it was dumb and avoided it for weeks for fear of feeling silly. Eventually, I decided to give it a go, although with a somewhat dismissive mind. I didn't think that it could possibly help. The fact is, much to my surprise, it really does help.

It's actually something I still do today. This is my confession! I am one of those *"Look in the mirror and tell yourself, you're special"* people. I know, it may seem terrible, and if you know me in real life it may even seem unbelievable, but it's the truth. It is not a huge part of my life, and it is not something that I rely on heavily anymore, but it is something that I used to help me get over my anxiety, and it is something that continues to help me to this very day. The best part is you don't have to actually mean it at first! This is one of the very few times you will ever hear me advising anyone to *"fake it, until you make it!"*

It took a little while to start taking mirror affirmations seriously. Like anything in life, the more you do it, the easier it becomes. Very soon it became a natural part of my day.

Overcoming The Real Problem

Social anxiety is a real problem. Some people dismiss it as just being shy which is both very wrong and totally unfair. Even a mild case of social anxiety is a *real* problem that can get worse over time if it is not addressed. The thing you must remember is that you can't let it be an excuse to ruin your life. The severity of your social anxiety is going to determine the time it takes you to become comfortable with looking people in the eyes. I still occasionally worry about it today, but what you eventually realize is that a little bit of manageable fear is a good thing; it keeps you on your toes.

You are going to hear me say **practice** numerous times in this book, so I am going to say it differently for you right now. You need to **participate in progressive desensitization** – I know, not the most snappy name! Progressive desensitization. This large, important sounding scientific term just means that you need to practice. Practice looking at people while you talk to them. With eye contact, the more you practice, the less sensitive you are to it. You get used to it. The brain no longer sees it as a threat. The more you do something, the easier it gets, as difficult as that sounds at the start.

Things To Remember

- Smile! Nothing is more effective than a smile. It warms your face, improves your eye contact and releases positive endorphins.

- Find focal points to draw into the conversation.

- Understand your face. Discover how it feels when you do different expressions.

Body Language – These Skills Change Everything

"The human body is the best picture of the human soul."
Ludwig Wittgenstein

Of course the early twentieth-century philosopher Wittgenstein was not referring directly to body language when he said these words, but they are helpful when we think about the role the body plays in conversation. Other people can only see what you present to them. They don't know about your rich inner life. They don't know about the grades that you received in school or the awards that you've won. They don't know about your failures and your successes, your bad times and your good. The people that you are attempting to engage in conversation only see the things that are right in front of them at that moment.

Let me ask you this: do you feel that people often misinterpret how you how feel during a conversation?

I used to feel this all the time. My friends would say such things as *"are you okay?"* or *"what's wrong?"* when they were talking with me. For a long time, I wondered what was wrong with people that they kept asking me these questions. Some people seemed to think I was angry about something while others thought I wanted to leave the situation I was in. The common theme was that they were misunderstanding me. They did not understand that I was just a bit socially anxious and felt very awkward in certain situations.

My nervous energy and my jittery movements implied to them that something else was wrong, or even worse that I just didn't want to talk to them anymore. I would often lie awake in bed at night and wonder why all these people were reading me so wrong. The answer should have been very clear, but it took me years to really discover it. In all of these conversations, situations, and scenarios where people would misunderstand me, the only common factor running through all of them was **me**. Slowly over time, the truth became clear. The way I carried myself was the problem.

This may seem like a fairly obvious observation now, but until you take that step back and look at yourself, you often can't see it. One of the hardest things you will ever do in your life is take a long hard look at yourself and analyze what you see with abject honesty. It is something that we all hate to do, but it is something that we all *need* to do at some point in our lives. You really might be shocked at what you learn!

Actions vs. Words

"What you do speaks so loud that I cannot hear what you say."
Ralph Waldo Emerson

I am going to digress here for a minute. I briefly want to discuss taking action in life. Dialogue is something that people engage in to enact change, in small or large ways. In other words, most of the time people are talking to you to get something accomplished. If you are consistently not taking action after the conversation, then this may affect how that person sees you.

I put this in the section on Body Language because I see this as a way that you are speaking to people with your entire person. By not acting on the things that you talk about doing, you are showing people you are not genuine.

I have been guilty of this several times in my life. I can still remember when I heard from a guy I was dating that my aunt had called me a "flake" - this was twenty years ago, and it still stings!

The guy worked with my aunt which is how I initially met him. After we started dating my aunt pulled her aside one day and said: *"You need to stay away from my niece, she's a flake."* Thanks, Auntie!

It hurt to hear, but when I look back at my life and all the plans that I had failed to follow through on, I understand what my aunt was trying to say. I needed to hear it. It was a kick in the butt, but it may have just been the kick in the butt that I needed. I had gotten to a place in my life where I was out of my comfort zone. I was afraid to make a move. I was letting fear rule my life. I was making new and different plans for my future every single day because just thinking about it and making lists was so much easier than actually **doing something**.

So, I guess the advice here is be a doer! If you say you will do something, then try to follow through. Do not make too many false promises.

The Key To Changing Your Social Skills

This is the magic section of the book where I give you the key to taking over any room with your posture. Don't worry this is not going to turn into one of those books that promises you your world will change if you start chanting a word and standing with one foot pointed towards the person you want to impress or anything utterly ridiculous like that! We can be much more subtle about it.

During the 80's and 90's many mindset books came out, with the majority of them being, quite frankly, cons. Several of them suggested that you should hold your hands in a triangle in front of you and smile widely to seem powerful. Many said you need to lean forward and encroach on people's personal space. And in some very small ways, they are actually correct. This really is one way to try and take over a room but you should realize you will be taking it over in a very negative and manipulative way. Yes, people may listen to you to a certain extent. However, you will look obnoxious, and the truth is they are likely only listening because they think it is the quickest way to get you to leave! They certainly will not want to talk to you again.

The old thinking on body language gave people all sorts of weird positions to try and contort themselves into. The new thinking on body language offers us something a little different but a lot more effective! New body language expert *Janine Driver*, claims that the new body language relies on staying natural and relaxed. In her best selling book *"You Say More Than You Think: Use the New Body Language to Get What You Want "* she says that *"It's about experiencing life."* which is very true. The key is experiencing it in a way where you are staying cognizant of how your body reacts to people, places, and things. You must not be ignorant of these factors.

Being aware of your body will help you deal with people. It will also help you to interpret these signals in other people. This is going to be a huge help to your overall communication skills. You'll know that when other people fold their arms, they are becoming defensive.

You'll know that they are fidgeting and checking their watch because they *might* be bored. You may see them sweating or shaking which is likely to mean they are anxious about trying to have the conversation and doubting their own skills.

Natural body language is the key. If you're not a hand talker, don't try to force it. Nothing looks more awkward than forced hand talking. It is like watching a toddler's karate demonstration. The best part of the new body language is that you don't have to change much about how you move when you talk. It is about being subtle.

Proper posture is very important. People look awful when they slouch. They look sad, and no one wants to talk to someone who looks sad. So do your best to stand up straight. Roll your shoulders back and slightly puff your chest out. Just doing this will make you appear more confident. You will look stronger and younger than you do when you slouch. It is the quickest way to change your appearance. Looking more confident will automatically and subconsciously make you *feel* more confident. The two go hand in hand.

Journaling Cue: Take a minute to yourself and stand up straight. How does it make you feel? Can you feel any changes?

This may seem like a slightly bizarre question but as a person who used to slouch, standing up straight was a huge change for me. Try it for yourself. When you stand up straight, does it change how you see yourself? Does it change how you feel about yourself? For a while, it made me quite self-conscious to walk around with my shoulders back, and my head held high, but it is worth fighting through these moments of potential embarrassment when you see the positive benefits at the end.

It is something that you need to train yourself to do. If you aren't used to standing up straight, it may take some time, but it is worth it. Personally, I would recommend yoga to help with this. Not only is it hugely beneficial for posture, it can have the added bonus of helping with weight loss. I had a potbelly for years, and that weight literally pulled me down. I am not a work out virtuoso, but through the use of YouTube yoga videos I have lost my potbelly and strengthened my back so that I can stand with perfect posture. I am actually an inch taller than I always thought I was!

Due to improving my overall posture, I look and feel ten years younger, and that has made a world of difference to how I feel about myself and how other people interact with me.

Reading Other People and How To Easily Respond To Them

Body language is a much talked about subject. A wealth of material exists both in book format and on the Internet. Unfortunately, a lot of this advice is at best inaccurate and unhelpful and at worst seriously detrimental to your communication skills.

Therefore I thought it would be valuable to break down the typical article on body language for you right now. I hope this will save you time and also help you avoid some of the nonsense that is out there such as this example from the website *Business Insider*.

"Worry, surprise or fear can cause people to raise their eyebrows in discomfort. So if someone compliments your new hairstyle or outfit with raised eyebrows, that person may not be sincere."

This passage has put a direct link between raised eyebrows and the confirmation of worry, surprise, fear, and insincerity. Apparently, there are a lot of messages that are being sent by these eyebrows.

Another quote from the same website reads *"In an attempt to avoid looking shifty-eyed, some liars will purposefully hold their gaze a touch too long so that it's slightly uncomfortable."*

While the above quotes might be true to *some* extent, equally, it could also be that the person is nervous, or filled with social anxiety. They may have just read one of the silly articles I talked about in the last chapter about how long to hold someone's gaze for.

The article pitches itself as a set of hard and fast rules for a topic where hard and fast rules lead to confusion. Body language is just not that simple.

Read The Signals

You are constantly sending out signals. It is impossible to stop it. However, simply being aware of the signals you are sending out can help you address the more negative ones. This is one side of the coin.

The other side of the coin is you also have to understand the signals that other people are putting out there. It can be very easy to obsess over ourselves and what we are doing or saying, but by only doing this we are in danger of missing some vital information that the other person is putting across. If a person wants to talk to you, they are going to be engaged. They will be listening actively, and they will be standing in a posture that is open to ideas.

A person standing in front of you with their arms crossed, or looking at their phone, is likely not ready or in the mood to have a conversation with you. The most important thing to remember is that this is okay. You are going to run into people who don't want to talk. No matter how good you get at the art of conversation, it takes two to tango. The other person has to be receptive, or you are just wasting your breath. You can't win them all! This is not a reflection on you. If you are open to conversation and you are trying to engage, then this one is on them. There are mean people everywhere, and as my friends bumper sticker says, *"Mean People Suck!"*.

The first step in reading someone is what the experts call *"Baselining."* Before you can know whether a person is reacting negatively or positively to your words, you have to know what they normally look like. This can take a little time. It is usually during the small talk portion of the conversation that you establish their baseline facial and body expressions.

For example, when you ask them about the weather, this is a great opportunity to gather baseline information. There's nothing exciting about the weather, unless a hurricane just rolled through. Once you have observed their behavior regarding the weather, you can introduce new topics that may elicit a response.

"Are you a Jays fan?"

"What do you think about the current election?"

Sports and politics are two subjects that can usually get a response. You can try from there to introduce new topics and watch for the changes in body posture, and gesture. It's like a game of poker, each person that you talk to has *'a tell.'*

When I worked in sales, I would use this technique all the time. It is a great way to try and find out who in the family makes the decisions. I would start by asking questions about the house, and family photos that might be on display. I would try my best to put everyone at ease. In this situation, it normally took me about ten minutes to get a baseline. I was a stranger coming into their house. I had to reassure them that I wasn't a serial killer.

Once I had the baseline, I could move on. I had one husband tell me that he made the decisions, but whenever I talked about money his eyes immediately shot over to his wife. I would talk about any other subject, and his eyes were focused on me, his posture relaxed. The second I mentioned price the eyes would go right to his wife. It was clear to me that this man was not the financial decision maker.

Not all tells are as easy to read. They are almost never universal. Even though body language is different for different people, there are four zones that you need to watch. Thankfully these zones are fairly simple to remember; head and shoulders, knees, and toes! When you are trying to find a baseline, checking all of these zones is important. Something as seemingly insignificant as a jittery foot can say as much as a nod for some people.

To try this out and get used to doing it, I would suggest you begin with family and close friends. You want to get used to doing it before you roll this out to the general public. It can look and feel a little unnatural at first; you don't always peer at a person's feet during a conversation! (well, I hope so anyway!)

I would never promise that you could solve every problem is a few seconds just by learning how to read people, but understanding these few basic things will *help* your conversations skills immensely. Even just having a heightened awareness of the other person is going to assist you as you attempt to engage in the art of conversation.

Things To Remember

- Stand tall.

- Use relaxed, natural gestures.

- Find the other person's baseline.

- Watch for the non-verbal cues. They can tell you so much.

You could go much further into reading body language if you want to but this is really as far as we need to go to for conversational body reading. You just want to be aware of how the other person is receiving your attempt to have a conversation. Most of us can see the extreme reactions. It's the subtle signs that often escape us. Being more aware of the signals will help to uncover the subtle messages that can make all the difference to a conversation.

Romantic Skills For The Shy

As I researched this chapter, I sifted through thousands of magazine articles that talk about body language tricks that supposedly help you uncover a person's romantic interest in you. Some of these articles were helpful and true; unfortunately **many** were not!

Every person has their own unique tricks and habits that reveal their secrets and desires, but to a certain extent, it is possible to generalize when it comes to romantic signals, both giving our own and reading other peoples.

Preening

Preening, which could be anything from fixing your hair to slightly arranging your clothes, is an ancient body language technique, directly passed down from the apes. Have you ever watched a wildlife program where monkeys and apes will preen their hair while in the company of a potential mate? Humans very much do the same thing, and it is a strong indicator to the other person that attraction is present.

Imitation

There is a very good reason why people say *"imitation is the highest form of flattery"*. Copying or seeing other people copy your moves (such as fixing your hair, moving your chair at an angle, scratching your arm etc.) is a subconscious way of telling or being told that the other person likes you. This is one of the most common romantic body language techniques, but also the one that is missed quite often.

Leaning In

If someone leans in towards you, they are basically saying *"I like you. I want to be closer to you"*. Leaning in can be with your whole body, or it can be something more subtle such as leaning your head towards the other person.

Touching The Other Person

This is one move you really have to show a little caution and good judgment with. Obviously be careful of where you are touching the other person! Generally, a light tap on the arm or hand when making a point or when walking together is quite an acceptable form of physical flirting but be sure the other person is standing or sitting close to you before attempting this. The fact they have chosen to be near to you will indicate they are already comfortable with you being in their physical space.

Pointing

By this I do not mean pointing with your finger, rather I mean pointing with a foot, knee or even your head. If the other person is sitting cross-legged, look at what their foot is doing. Is it pointing towards you? This is quite a common way for a person to flirt using body language. Like a lot of these points, it is often subconscious.

Eye Contact

Lingering eye contact is a good way of flirting, but often people have difficulty understanding the difference between the other person just being interested in the conversation and flirting. A good way to tell if the person is actually flirting is to watch their eye contact Does their gaze flit from one eye to the other? If so then you can take that as a very strong sign that attraction is there!

Reading Different Types of People

I have already discussed how we are all different and therefore it can be difficult to generalize too much when it comes to body language. Gestures can differ across ethnic, religious, and cultural lines. Personal space expectations are not the same across all cultures, in fact, they can often be vastly different; for example, people from the Middle East stand much closer to each other than people from London or New York.

Again this is why the concept of base-lining is so vitally important. People are not one-size-fits-all, and we should not expect them to be.

When it comes to body language, my biggest advice would be to simply get out there and do it. Watch other people. See how they move. See how their body reacts when they are angry and see how different it is when they are relaxed and happy. Over time this analysis will become more and more natural and less of something you actually need to think about. Reading body language without overthinking is something that can only be mastered with practice…and yet more practice.

Movements In Daily Life

This short exercise is concerned with understanding the movements you make in your daily life. Knowledge can directly lead us to the opportunity to change and to grow.

For this brief exercise, you will need a pen, paper, and a mirror…but the most important thing you will need is your absolute honesty. This honesty must be in both your body motions and honesty in your descriptions and feelings. You are going to try to describe the motions that your body goes through in different situations.

It might be good to try this exercise with a partner, but even if you do, I recommend you still use a mirror too. Your aim is to describe your own movements, but you will have the other person there to create a real-life conversation, and you can watch yourself react to the social situation in the mirror. The other person could also help to keep you honest and true to yourself.

Steps:

- Think of an emotion. This could be anger, joy, sadness, shyness etc.

- Talk out loud about this emotion. Try accurately and honestly express it.

- Carefully watch your movements in the mirror. Notice how you are sitting or standing. Notice your hands. Your feet. Your mouth. Notice how you are moving your head as you speak.

- Now take a few minutes and begin to write down what you see. Try to be quite open at this part, write down honestly what you see and any surprising things you might notice. This could be something as simple as you crossing your arms when you began to speak or perhaps lack of smiling or eye contact.

- Repeat this exercise again with the next emotion.

Once you've tried this on yourself, you need to move on to other people and how you see them. Perhaps you have a partner or a close friend who would be willing to help you out with this? If you don't, you can use a movie. A 'realistic' drama would likely be best. Take your time and flesh out your descriptions. I realize that not everyone likes to write, but your skill to create beautiful prose is not what this is about. It's just a way to get you thinking more about bodies and the ways that they communicate. Many people are surprised about just how effective this exercise is, but again it really does rely on you being honest and open in order for it to be successful.

Moving On

The mechanics of a conversation are literally the hardest thing to master when it comes to speaking with people. Difficult, maybe, but most definitely not impossible. You don't have a mirror in front of you when you speak to people. You aren't able to see yourself through other people's eyes, and it is very difficult to get constructive feedback, especially from complete strangers. Therefore it will take some work, dedication and above all patience on your behalf in order to make this a success.

The best advice is also the most basic; **get out and talk to people.** I have read so many advice columns and scholarly texts about the proper amounts of time, and the optimum number of blinks per second you should do when in a conversation. That is fine for a book, but it does not work like that in real life. If you are sitting across from someone trying to figure out how many times you are blinking, then I can absolutely guarantee that you are not having a *real* or in any way productive conversation. It would be impossible to actually be present in the moment.

Use the exercises I have provided and keep the advice in mind, but the only way to master these skills is to actually use them, ideally on a daily basis. Talk to as many people as you can. Don't be afraid to fail, you are going to many times before you succeed, and that is okay.

We now have all of the skills necessary to have a meaningful conversation. Your face, eyes, ears, and body are ready to continue on our journey.

Part Two – You vs Work

Together we have already gone over the mechanics of conversation. So how do you take these lessons and apply them to the workplace? Conversation is an important part of any profession. From the interview to the presentation, it plays an important role. Even within the ever-changing politics of the office, there are many hurdles to go through as you climb the company ladder.

However, it should be made clear that the lessons I am going to teach you can apply to ANY area of your life. I am going to focus on work in this section as this makes it easier to give examples, but the advice, tips, and steps can be used in your life in general.

Studies show that the workplace is one place where an introvert usually suffers most and can often produce the most anxiety. Your shyness can really hold you back from fulfilling your full potential. Co-workers, who perhaps don't work nearly as hard as you do, can often get promoted ahead of you because they are not afraid to speak up. Being introverted, in many cases, means you're working twice as hard for half the pay.

More importantly, it is affecting your health. Stress is a killer. If you are sitting around the office all day worried that you might have to talk to people or give a presentation, it is going to lead to all sorts of health problems. When you are anxious for any length of time, you are going to feel it all over your body.

When I first entered the working world, I took a bunch of low paying jobs. I didn't want to talk to people. I felt shy, anxious and awkward. As I moved into sales, and then management, I realized that I was still suffering from my shyness. Stress was leading to ulcers and high blood pressure. I was still a very young woman, but I was dealing with very serious health issues related to my issues with other people. I had to change many things including my diet to deal with these issues.

However, during this time I also learned a great deal about myself, and about the art of business conversation. The office can be a dangerous place, especially for the new guy or girl. One of the keys to business success is negotiating your way through office politics. There is also the boardroom and dreaded parties. I am going to cover it all in the next section, but it all starts with the interview.

Dealing With Job Interviews

"I had a job interview at an insurance company once and the lady said 'Where do you see yourself in five years?' and I said 'Celebrating the fifth year anniversary of you asking me this question'"
Mitch Hedberg

This is a book about having a conversation but as pointed out by job site monster.com *"many job seekers fail to recognize that often the best interviews don't feel as much like interviews as they do compelling conversations."*

This is a great way to approach your job interview. If you go in there waiting to be grilled, you are going to be on the defensive, but a conversation has a more balanced power structure. Framing it in this way is going to help you stay relaxed at a time when a little composure can go a long way.

The same rules apply to a job interview as apply to a conversation. You need to start with small talk. Engage the interviewer by asking about some of the pictures or knick-knacks in his or her office. *"Are you a Seahawks fan? How are they looking this year?"*.

This is where you'll grab your baseline. Body language cues can be extremely useful especially when you're trying to assess how the interview is going.

There are certain situations that demand eye contact. A job interview is one of these times. As the interviewee, you need to impress upon the interviewer that you are confident, trustworthy and that you can effectively do the job. The interview is one of those social situations where your body is saying as much as your words, and good eye contact is where it all starts. This is a common piece of advice that you will hear, for very good reasons.

Luckily for you, you've already read the chapter on eye contact, so you know all about how to make eye contact, and you've practiced ways to make your eye contact more effective. That's going to help you out a lot.

But wait! Oh no! You just got into the room, and there are two people who are conducting the interview. Who do you look at?

The answer is very simple. You look at both of them. This should make the job of avoiding staring even easier. The more eyes there are in the room, the less contact each one of them should be expecting. Spread the eye contact around. Make sure to start each answer by looking at the person who asked the question. Acknowledge that it is their question that you are answering and then move your way through the other interviewers as you elaborate.

People will spend a lot of time practicing their handshake for a job interview. They think that they need a special one. I have practiced my handshake many times over the years. I use the same one in every situation. The firm confident handshake works in every situation. Trying to make it extra firm, or the smile extra confident just for the job interview is going to make you seem awkward and unnatural. Find a handshake that works for you, and use it every time. Once you've settled on a handshake and committed to it, muscle memory takes care of the rest.

Preparing a special handshake, or different rules of eye contact is just going to make it harder to appear natural. The more relaxed you are, the more natural you are going to seem. Try not to put too much pressure on yourself. While there are certain things that you have to be ready for on a job interview, try to stay as natural as possible.

How To Easily Answer Questions

An interview is often, unfortunately, a little more structured than everyday conversation. Sometimes it may feel like HR departments have developed their own language. The questions may seem coded and after they are asked the interviewer waits for the proper Pavlovian response. Asking us questions like: **"if you were a tree,**

what kind of tree would you be?" *(Yes, a friend did actually get that question once in an interview! What kind of a question is that?!)*

I have been on both sides of a job interview, and I can say with absolute certainty that there is no formulaic answer you can give to *any* question that will guarantee you a job. The answer that works for one person may not work for you. Therefore your answers need to be genuine and natural.

I am not saying that practicing answering interview questions is pointless. You need to be relaxed when you apply for a job. To be relaxed, you need to be prepared. You can only control what you can control, which comes down to you. Your level of preparedness is something that you can *absolutely* control. So do as many prep questions as possible. Get your answers ready, but be aware you may need to answer questions you have not prepared for. Doing the prep questions is more about you trying to *feel* ready, than actually predicting what the interviewer is going to ask.

The prep is about getting you into the right mindset to answer the real questions. As I mentioned early, try to relate the answer to the position. Do this with each one of your prep questions and get used to relating the answers to the position. Here is a quick example.

Interviewer: Do you see yourself as a leader or a follower?

Me: I am a leader who knows how to listen. During my years working in customer service, I have learned how to listen to people but to hear more than their words. I know that their complaints are not always directly related to the complaints that they are voicing. Using keen leadership skills, I can find a solution that goes beyond what they were expecting.

I laid it on thick in that answer. Thick can work. Thick can also turn people off. This is where your body language reading skills are going to come in. Watch the interviewer's response and look for the cues to help you determine how far you can go with your answers.

Journaling Cue: Answer the previous interview question and relate them to the job you wish you had.

Think about why you make a good candidate for this job, and what you hope to accomplish in this position?

Talking About Yourself

"Tell me about yourself!"
Whenever I hear this in an interview or at a party, I have this bizarre fear it may be a trap. I know I am not alone in having trepidation about this question.

The tendency is to actually tell the interviewer about yourself, and because you're nervous, you ramble. *"I like surfing and nacho chips, but only with real cheese none of that plastic stuff. I like long walks on the beach..."*

You have to stop.
Take a breath.
Take a second.
Think about the job that you're applying for and the qualities that the company is looking for in their ideal candidate. They likely listed these qualities in the job description. Use this as your guide.

Testing Your Answering Skills

You will have likely heard of the mock interview before. Some people dismiss this as they can feel silly but it can be a very powerful thing. The same principles can be used for having a mock conversation in order to practice more general communication skills. However I want you to do something different – I want *you* to be the interviewer and to conduct the mock interview.

I recommend that you do the interview, you ask the questions, and therefore you get to experience this side of it. Try to put yourself in the position of being an interviewer. Imagine that you own a business and you are trying to find the right person to fill this position.

Exercise Steps:

- Think of a real job position to fill.

- Write down all of the qualities you would be looking for in that person.

- Research the qualifications that a person would need to fill the position.

- Conduct the interview.

This is an amazing way to prepare yourself for a job interview. You are putting yourself in the other person's shoes, and this can give you a valuable and unique insight into the process.

Flipping the Script

"Finding a job that is a good fit is as much about you selecting the right company as it is about them selecting the right candidate."
Miles Anthony Smith

When you are applying for a job anywhere, you need to realize that they need you too. Some people walk into a job interview and immediately give all of the conversational power over to the interviewer. They are approaching the interview as a person willing to do *anything* to work for the company. People can smell desperation and the interviewer is not going to be impressed. The same principle applies to general communication. If you appear so desperate to get on with the other person that you just mindlessly agree with everything they say, the other people will find it difficult to respect you.

You need to approach the interview or conversation with a different mindset. You are not desperate; you can get a job anywhere. I'm not asking you to use these exact words, but this is the energy you need to put out. Ask about the company's benefit plans, and the creature comforts that the employees are afforded.

Make them impress you! In an economy where employees are constantly searching for the job that is offering the most incentives, the workers have the power. The company needs you, or they wouldn't have placed the ad. Always remember that they need you as much as you need them. The same principle applies to everyday life.

Let your power come through. It's an attitude. A confident smile. A head held high. A firm handshake. Allow yourself to believe that you have the power. Allow the power to flow through you and the interviewer will feel it too.

Pulitzer Prize-winning author Alice Walker once said, *"The most common way people give up their power is by thinking they don't have any."*

Do not give up your power. Not for anyone.

Making Friends At Work and At Home

"I always arrive late at the office, but I make up for it by leaving early."
Charles Lamb

Playing office politics is a dangerous game. Engaging in politics within circles of friends can be disastrous.

Every time you put people in a room together, there is an immediate 'sorting' that happens. We naturally start to develop relationships with the people who we are forced to be around. An office, or any workplace, is always going to be filled with cliques and groups. As a newcomer, it is up to you to sniff out these dynamics and find your place in the workplace society. The same is true when you join a sports club, start a new hobby or begin to socialize with a different group of people.

When you first walk into an office, it can feel like a hostile environment. This is especially true if you're being put into a management position. You are the newcomer, and you may be walking into a very tightly knit group that is still loyal to the old manager, or the outgoing employee you are replacing.

So how do you navigate this minefield? Set boundaries with your new co-workers or friends. As a shy person in my past, I found myself turning to people-pleasing to get people to like me. I wanted to be liked. We *all* like to be liked. It's a part of the human condition. It is perfectly natural to feel this way.

The reality is, these situations are not always easy to handle. It is hard to know what to say, how to behave, how to please one person but not offend someone else…the list goes on and on. It is hard to establish barriers and bridges with a co-worker or friend. Every relationship has unwritten rules.

Knowing What You Want – And Knowing How To Get It

It may appear difficult to avoid getting sucked into the vortex of office politics or drama with friends. People are naturally drawn to drama. Perhaps you feel you are constantly being dragged into stressful dramatic situations more than most people? If so then ask yourself this; do you know how you always find yourself stuck in the middle of it?

Knowing what you want is a very important thing in life, and never more important than when you're working in an office. Decide right now how emotionally invested you are in the place where you work. Is this job a stepping stone? Is this your forever job? Why did you come into work today? Be honest.

Journaling Cue: What are you trying to accomplish in your current employment position?
Is this a stepping stone job?
Are you just passing the time until something better comes along?

I want you to really think about the place where you work and the impact that you are going to let office politics have on your life. Going back to interview questions, is this where you see yourself in five years? If not, why are you letting this place stress you out?

Once you've answered these questions for yourself, you can decide how much of yourself you're going to allow the people in the office to have. Are you going to play their games, or are you going to fight back? These are the things you need to know before you make a plan for overcoming the hurdles of dealing with office politics.

Navigating Close and Not Close Friends

When you got to work…you are there to **work**. The people at your place of work do not need to be your friends. They are your co-workers. We all want people to like us. This is a natural feeling. However, you must face the, somewhat harsh reality, that not everyone is going to like you. It is impossible! We have to get past that!

Knowing and accepting this will help you avoid dealing with the political predators roaming the halls, and hunting people at the water coolers. You will also have the confidence of knowing that if conflict does arise you have all of your work done. It is the same advice you would get if you became a Boy Scout; be prepared! There is a certain amount of security and confidence that comes from being prepared. People will feel and recognize the confidence you project, and they will be more unlikely to drag you into drama.

The Power Of NO!

"Half of the troubles of this life can be traced to saying yes too quickly and not saying no soon enough."
Josh Billings

You want everyone to like you, but who is going to like you if you say yes to way too many people and then you can't deliver on any of it? I have made this mistake more than once. I thought it made me seem like a *'go getter.'* I wanted to appear super-organized and dependable, but in reality, I ended up looking lazy and untrustworthy!

You can't do everything. You need time to sleep. You need time to get your own work done. This is another place where office politics come into play. What if you finish a favor for one person, but you don't complete the project that somebody else asked you to undertake?

Saying '**YES**' is easy. All too easy at times, which can lead to a lot of issues and stress further down the line.

Saying '**NO**' is a skill that could literally change your life. I understand that you do not want to hurt people's feelings. You want to make sure that they know why you are saying no. Give them a reason. You have a job to do too. Your social life is too busy this week. You have family commitments. You don't want to insult anyone. You need to be firm, but polite.

Your Own Feelings

You need to be happy with yourself before you can be happy in an office or any other social setting.

If you are looking for your happiness externally in other people, you will never be happy. Other people are not responsible for giving you the happiness, or the peace you are looking for. Fleeting moments of happiness maybe, but that is it. That is all they are capable of giving you. Real and lasting happiness has to come from you.

Make sure you take the time that you need for yourself. Do not let your job or your social life control how you feel about yourself. Take time for yourself every day. Go and do a workout at lunch. Meditate on your breaks if that is what makes you happy. Wander around the shops on your own. It doesn't matter what it is, just make sure you take some time for yourself during the day.

Your new found conversation skills are going to help with all of this. Proper communication skills can help you avoid the pitfalls of social and office politics. You will be able to read people and see what they are really trying to get out of you. You will make that all important, *'good first impression'* and that is going to let people know that they cannot walk all over you. Conversation skills and confidence are the first and main steps in the foundations of lasting happiness.

Dealing With Parties!

Whether it is Christmas party with friends or a cocktail party for new clients, there are certain rules that you should follow when you are speaking to people at a party. I have a more comprehensive section on small talk later in the book, but it should be clear that a work party is a very different situation from a casual friends party.

At one of my first every office parties, I thought that a few cocktails would help me loosen up. The nerves made me drink more. And then a bit more again. I don't remember much about that night, but I do remember one very clear moment when my boss pulled me aside.

"Touch my lips," he said to me. I was really freaked out, and I was wondering what HR would think about this request, but I did it. *"They're dry,"* he said. *"At a cocktail party, drinks are for holding, not for drinking."* He told me that he never spoke to anyone for long enough for them to notice that he was just holding his drink and not consuming it. I never forgot that advice, and cocktail parties were actually much easier after that point.

You may think it is fine to get drunk at casual parties with friends, but this can also lead to serious consequences if you are nervous. Drinking and anxiety do ***not*** mix well. Drinking alcohol is really only a good idea when you are in a safe place, emotionally, physically, and geographically. Any other time it can lead to disaster. If you're anxious before you start drinking, the alcohol is going to hit you differently than if you're not. I realize it is the same product, but it interacts with your body differently at different times.

Alcohol is always a wildcard, or I should say, **you** mixed with alcohol is a wildcard! We always think we know, but we're never really a hundred percent sure how it's going to hit us. It's much better to just face the party without it or with just a small amount. The risk can be too great. As a shy person, relying on alcohol can be a dangerous crux.

Journaling Cue: What has Alcohol helped you accomplish in life?

Be honest with yourself. If you have an example, write it out and try to think of specifically how the alcohol helped. Ask yourself if you might have been able to accomplish this goal more efficiently when sober?

In college, I had a class at 8:30 am every Friday morning. After my first class in this time slot, I realized that the other students were all drinking on Thursday nights. It was a big thing at the time. Bars were offering cheaper prices and Thursday night drinking really took off. This had one mammoth bonus for me - I walked into all of these classes looking like a genius.

Not drinking on Thursday nights allowed me to be fresher, more alert, and generally find it easier to participate in the classes. The same is true for normal social events. Not being the drunken or hangover mess can put you at a large advantage.

I should make it very clear that I am not totally against alcohol. I drink and enjoy it. If dealt with correctly it can be a great way to help you let go and have fun or relax after a long week. You just need to ensure you do not rely on it and learn how to handle it when you do drink.

Personally, I don't want to be dependent on anything. I want to be in control of my own destiny. If you feel like you need alcohol to communicate with others, then that is just another thing to worry about which can lead to even more serious issues down the road. It is another strike against your confidence. Break the dependence and learn to talk to people without alcohol playing a role.

How To Be Assertive

"Being president is like running a cemetery: you've got a lot of people under you and nobody's listening."
Bill Clinton

This is a President who knew what he was talking about. Especially when it came to leadership. This is a tricky situation to be in. You have navigated your way through the interview, the office politics, and the awkward presentations. Or, alternatively, you have found your way through the difficult path of friendship, meeting someone new, hanging out with a new crowd. And now you find yourself in a position of power.

There is no question that you have to change the way you talk to people when you are in a position of power. Suddenly all of your words have weight to them. Your very presence carries a different meaning on the office floor or at the dinner party.

Can a person who suffers from shyness be a good leader both at work and in everyday life Absolutely, yes! Study after study shows that this is more than possible.

My former shyness meant I spent a lot of my time listening. My journey to overcome shyness has made me more acutely aware of people and how they communicate. I have learned how to project courage and how to inspire it in others. I know that anyone reading this book can accomplish these things too.

As a naturally shy person, who is more comfortable listening than talking, I am at an advantage. Sometimes the best thing to say is actually nothing. Being an active and engaged listener shows your employees, or those who work under you, that you care about their opinions. The better you are at listening and making them comfortable, the more you will learn about them, and the job that they do. It is important to build this trust and get your underlings to open up to you. It will breed a healthier work environment.

I made an effort to learn about communicating to try and understand the message that I was sending out to people. I wanted to know why I felt I could be quite off-putting sometimes. During this process, I learned a ton about the things that people are telling you without using words. Reading people has been an incredibly useful tool as a leader.

Leadership guru Simon Sinek claims that good leaders start with **why**. In his best-selling book, *"Start with Why: How Great Leaders Inspire Everyone to Take Action",* Sinek tells us that the greatest leaders and innovators of our time all started with the question why. Steve Jobs, Martin Luther King, and even the Wright brothers. They innovated and revolutionized the way we experience the world with this simple question.

This same advice can be used in your everyday life. Why? Why spend time with that person and not someone else? Why do a job you hate when you could possibly find a job you love? Why be stuck in an unhappy rut in life, when you could strive for better? Why?

Journaling Cue: What is your why?

Maybe you don't run a multi-million dollar business, and maybe you aren't in management, but what is your why? What is the thing that is driving your actions professionally or personally? If you can't think of a why, maybe this is something that you need to take a deeper look at.

So how does this apply to having a conversation? When you know the *why*, then you are prepared to face the questions and the struggles of leadership or deal with complicated personal relationships.

Being a leader, in any respect, means having all types of different conversations. In each situation, a calm demeanor, which is both open and firm, is going to help make the conversation easier to handle on both sides.

When you are a leader in the workplace, it is important to understand that it is your responsibility to make your underlings feel comfortable. Once again, this is about finding a balance. You want them to feel comfortable enough to talk to you, but you do not have to be best buddies with everyone. The balance of power between employer and employee is very delicate. If they think of you as a friend, and vice-versa, it makes many of the interactions essential to this relationship more difficult.

Speaking Out Loud: Everything From Public Speaking to Making Small Talk!

"But I never could make a good impromptu speech without several hours to prepare it."
Mark Twain

Public speaking. Is there any part of communication that produces more fear and trepidation in the general public than public speaking? The professional public speaker Michael Mescon once said, *"The best way to conquer stage fright is to know what you're talking about."*

Or as an old boss of mine usually to constantly say; *"You have to do your due diligence."*

Both of these statements are very true. If you are properly prepared to give your speech or presentation, then you have done as much as can be expected of you. Relax, you have the knowledge you need, and you are ready to go.

The most important thing to remember is that no one is comfortable making a speech. Really. NOBODY! Being a little nervous and even blushing a bit in these situations is expected and nearly always forgiven. You need to remind yourself that in most cases you are going to be much harder on yourself than the people in the audience will be. The more preparation you have done, the better. You should know the topic you are speaking about very well and be able to go off on tangents if required. This applies as much to a conference as it does for a speech at a wedding or even telling a story to a group of people at a dinner party.

So, what can you do if you have done the research and put in the time, but you still feel nervous? I guess there is always the age-old advice of trying to picture everyone in their underwear! Aside from that, here are a few more helpful tips for speeches.

Go Big!

If you are using notes or a script, then ensure you print it out in a large font and double-spaced. I know you are killing trees, and I feel horrible about that, but you will be able to read your notes so much clearer, even if you are shaking. There is nothing worse than realizing you can't see your notes clearly or having to strain to see them, completely destroying the flow of your speech.

Take Control.

Do not be afraid to pause. Take a sip of your water. Wait for complete silence. Take a deep breath. Know that the room belongs to you, not the other way around. If you feel in control, you will feel confident. Those two feelings go hand in hand.

Laugh at Yourself.

People can't laugh at you if you beat them to it! Do not be afraid to laugh at your own slip-ups. Everyone makes mistakes, so why not just embrace them? It is the best tactic to get away with mess-ups and is regularly used by world leaders and celebrities. People will warm to you and immediately forgive any mistakes if you tackle it with a bit of self-depreciating humor.

Dress for Success.

Corny advice, sure, but it works! People respond to clothing, so dress in clothes that make you feel confident and make you feel good about yourself. Make sure you feel comfortable. If you can't breathe or move properly, that is going to affect your ability to deliver the speech to the best of your abilities.

Practice. And then practice some more.

If you are giving an actual speech, then practice, practice, practice. Deliver the speech just one more time! And then practice it again. Practice what you are going to say to family, friends, pets, or anyone who will listen to you! Nothing beats repetition for learning something to a comfortable and natural level.

Volunteer.

One of the best ways to be ready for a speech or to improve your public speaking skills is just to be used to going and talking to groups of people in less pressured situations. One way that you can do that is to volunteer at hospitals, fundraisers, or schools. In University I became a student ambassador. We gave tours of the University to potential, and incoming students. Their families usually came with them, and they were normally organized into large group tours. Of course, it was daunting at first, but in the long-term, this really helped me get over my fear of public speaking and taught me some very valuable lessons.

Presentations.
At some point in your life, you may have to give a presentation. This could be at a major event but it is more likely to be in a work environment in front of a handful of people. Even if you know these people well and work with them every day, standing up and giving an actual presentation is something that a lot of people find incredibly tough and even borderline terrifying. I know of two people who did not progress in their respective careers for the simple reason they avoided opportunities that may have meant them having to give a presentation in order to move up the ladder.

If the thought of giving a presentation is one that scares you, do not worry, you are not alone. Let's be realistic here, the fear may never *completely* leave you, you may always feel nervous going into these situations, but really, it can become manageable with some tips and advice.

Practice On Video Or With A Friend.
Do I need to remind you yet again of the power and effectiveness of practice when doing anything like this?

Once you have become semi-comfortable with practicing your presentation alone, the next step is to try it out in front of someone or if that is not possible then film yourself. At first, this can be incredibly difficult to get the courage to do, and you may even feel silly, but it is a very effective way of spotting what you is going well and what you need to improve upon. If you are performing this in front of a friend, ask them to be totally honest with you, otherwise, the exercise is pointless.

The Start & The End.
The two most vital parts of a successful presentation are the beginning and the end. When it comes to getting over your nerves, then the beginning is crucial. Spend more time on this part than anything else. If you can nail the start, your confidence will improve, and the presentation will flow better from there onwards. The first few minutes can be the toughest, especially if you have a presentation to set up. Trying to get a file to load, or setup a dry easel board that just won't go can sure increase the anxiety levels pretty damn fast so prepare for this as much as possible. You have to remember that what you're actually afraid of is the unknown. You can't control everything that is going to happen up there but control what you can. By this I mean you. Make sure your equipment is ready, and you know what you're going to say. You don't need to memorize the whole speech, but the opening minute or so should be committed to memory. Taking these steps will help you appear more confident as you feel out the room. The beginning is vital. If you nail that, then it is just a domino effect from there. Ask if you can be in the room before the audience or co-workers arrive, familiarize yourself with the surroundings and spend some time ensuring any props or slideshows you are using are as ready to go as possible.

Involve Your Audience.
This is a great tip both for dealing with your own nerves and for making the audience feel included, important and part of the talk. It can also help with bringing diminishing attention back to the presentation. Involving the audience does not have to be anything dramatic. It can be as simple as asking the audience a question, inviting them to ask you a question or asking for a show of hands on a particular point.

You Are Not Talking To A Busy Room!
This is something a lot of people I know do when they are nervous

about a presentation or a talk. Pick a friendly looking face in the audience. Talk at him or her for a minute before picking a new face and so on and so on. In this way, you will begin to feel you are talking to one person at a time and not a busy room. Just make sure you don't stare at the same person for too long!

You Are Not Alone.
Remember, fear of public speaking is one of the most common anxieties, and I don't just mean with shy people. I mean with everybody. You are not alone. You are not weird or odd or a freak to be nervous and scared of it. You are not unique in this. Many other people feel the same way, even if they sometimes hide it well.

Jokes Do Not Always Work.
A lot of books will advise you to crack a joke in order to get people to relax. While this may work with some people, the simple truth is many of us, myself included, do not find telling a joke a particularly easy or comfortable thing to do. Telling a joke can be very dangerous. There is always the chance that no one will get it. Even if you've told the joke a million times, there's a chance that this is going to be the audience that hates it. Unless you feel you are naturally funny, then I would advise you to steer clear of telling a joke. Injecting a little light-heartedness into the talk is perfectly fine though and can be very beneficial.

Writing A Formal Speech.
A speech or a presentation can be hard to sit down and prepare, and you may be suffering under the delusion that you can wing it and just make it up as you go along. Very few people in the world are capable of doing this to any decent standard, and I am most definitely not one of them. It is really not recommended! The more prepared you are, the more confident you will feel and appear. So take the time and write out your speech.

Organize your thoughts with a specific goal in mind. If you could boil the point of the speech down to one statement what would that be? That statement is your jumping off point. Once you know what you want to communicate to the audience than you can build the speech around that.

Attitude Matters.

When you are writing, and presenting a speech you first have to decide on the tone of the speech. What are you going to focus on? What are you trying to accomplish? If you are making a sales presentation, then you need to avoid the push. You want to convince people to buy your product, but avoid the pushiness of the hard-sell. If you are presenting data, you need to focus your effort on explaining how this data helps the people in your audience. If you are going to be attending a dinner party and want to practice telling a story, then you need to think about who may be attending, what age they are, what sort of humor is or isn't appropriate etc.

Be a giver on the stage, boardroom, coffee room, party, friends house or wherever you are. Deliver a speech that is focused on helping the audience and enriching their lives. Even if you are the focus of your presentation, you can still provide the information or speech in an open, honest, humble and giving way that will immediately bring the audience to your side.

Being Seen As Nervous.

According to the *Andrew Kukes Foundation for Social Anxiety,* one of the top 5 indicators of social anxiety in adults is a fear of being noticeably nervous to other people. In my own personal journey, this was one of the hardest things for me to try and get past. I was afraid of being sweaty, jittery and starting to blush…which would of course then make me sweaty, jittery, and start to blush! It was a vicious cycle and one that many people with shyness go through. For the shy person, this is as true for giving a talk as it is for attending a party or any other social event.

What you need to understand is people see you in a totally different light to what you might think. Do you really think they can see every little nervous tic you may do or the fact that you are starting to feel a bit hot and sweaty? And if they do…well…does it really matter? I know, I know, it is easy for me to say that, but do remember I was in your position once too. Some things can be helped with practical advice, and some things just need time, patience and effort to get over. You can get over this, just as I did.

Making Small Talk.
The ability to easily make small talk with people is a wonderful thing. It can open up a new world of possibilities. Many shy people struggle with this, as I once did in my past. How did I overcome my fear? Step by step, day by day.

The most important lesson I have ever learned about small talk is also the most simple: it does not matter *what* you say, it just matters that you say *something*.

Shyness and low self-esteem often go hand in hand. The shy person may feel inferior. They may feel they are not capable of being interesting, funny or captivating and that the other person will get bored of them immediately. This fear is because of low confidence and low self-esteem.

I advise you to do this: observe. Take some time over the next week and listen to people making small talk. This could be in an elevator, in the queue at the coffee shop or on the bus. Pay careful attention. What you will realize is, 99% of what they say *is* actually quite mundane stuff! How many people do you know make small talk by discussing politics or deep philosophical thinking? Nobody! People discuss the weather. Their day. The event they are at. How good the food is in the restaurant. How long the queue is. The list goes on.

Let go. Nobody, except yourself, is expecting you to discuss anything too deep or to be utterly fascinating or hilarious. Open your mind and speak. Remember this: it is called SMALL talk. Not big talk. **SMALL TALK!**

Journaling Cue: What have been your experiences with public speaking?

What has happened while you were speaking in public either in a formal setting or perhaps just telling a story at a dinner party? Be honest and open. Write down your experience; the good, the bad and the ugly. Remember you are writing this in a private journal. It is a safe place, only for you, unless you choose to let anyone else see it. Public speaking can be terrifying; there is no way around that. In my past, I have given speeches that I haven't even been able to hear, because of the sound of my heartbeat ringing in my ears. Things are so much better now, but believe me, I know how the fear feels. What have been your experiences of public speaking? What mistakes did you make? Are you being overly critical of yourself? What did you do right? Did you congratulate yourself for at least trying?

Assertiveness Is A Valuable Tool

"The way we communicate with others and ourselves ultimately determines the quality of our lives."
Tony Robbins

Assertiveness is not an overnight thing to achieve, but it is also not as impossible as you may have once thought. I hope you can take that away from this section of the book. I truly believe that you can make it, by employing the techniques that you have learned here.

I am also hoping that through a mastery of your fears and proper conversation skills you can find a better place for yourself on the work and social ladder. If you are not careful, it can be easy to find yourself being stepped on and walked over by more vocal. Always be aware that you *are* good enough. You are worthy. People should respect you.

Speaking to people in any professional setting can be difficult, and there is no way to completely get over the fears that you have overnight. You need to realize that whatever the change is that you want to make in your life, it is going to take effort on your part. Effort and patience. But I am here to tell you that it *is* worth it.

Part Three – Conversation Skills For Everyday Life

We have looked at the physical manifestation of the conversation and how to apply them in some areas of your life. Now we will cover how to use these skills in your everyday life. Conversations are not just about winning or looking good. Most importantly, they are about building lasting healthy relationships.

This section is going to walk you through the elements of personal conversation and how you can use it to, quite literally, change your life. When I look back at my life before I started to study the art of conversation, I can see I was often totally lost. There were so many opportunities that I missed and so many people that I lost the chance to get to know better or even at all. I wish that I had been able to connect with these people. These connections would have changed a lot for me.

Romantic connections, friendships, and human connections are a valuable resource for all people. Humans are social creatures. We need to interact with each other. It doesn't matter if you have a million friends or three, what matters is that you're able to connect with them on that deeper level.

"Deeper level" does, of course, mean a variety of things in different situations. For example, deeper level when dealing with a romantic connection is very different than when dealing with a friendship and in turn can be different again when dealing with a family member. Whatever the relationship is, you can feel the connection when you have it. I used to think that conversation and connecting were a lot of work, and truthfully at times, they can be. However, they are worth the effort, and I promise you, if you put in the effort and try the simple exercises that I have provided in this book, you will see a difference in your quality of life and the richness of the human connections you make throughout the rest of your life.

Making Introductions

I am talking about introductions in the broad sense of the word, to mean the beginning of a conversation. It is the opening of a dialogue, and it is your chance to get things started off on the right foot. However, do not feel you need to do anything dramatic here. I once spoke at a conference where one of the other speakers, who shall remain nameless, advised the audience to introduce themselves by bellowing out a **HELLO!** as loud as they possibly could, in order to really get the other persons attention. This is one piece of advice I most certainly do **not** recommend, not unless you want to frighten the other person!

The initial greeting, the first few words you say, should be kept simple, and humble. Do not try to do this with too much flair. A simple, confident hello with good eye contact and perhaps a handshake, if appropriate, is really all that is needed at this stage.

Once the initial greeting is out of the way, we move on to the introduction. This is pretty cut and dry. *"Hello, my name is So-and-so,"*. There doesn't need to be anything fancy about the way you say your name. The trick is to find ways to remember the *other* person's name when they say it. You only really have one or two times to try and rebound from forgetting a person's name before it becomes rude and shows a lack of respect for them.

I have a neighbor who has lived beside me for three years. I hope to God I never see him at a party or out anywhere. We talk almost every day, and he has already told me his name on at least four occasions. I can no longer ask this man his name. It is over. I know that one day my shame will come out, but I am trying to avoid it at all costs!

I do have a strategy for avoiding embarrassing situations like this, but it requires two people. You have to work out a signal so that non-verbally you can tell your partner that you don't know the person in question's name. Once the target is established, you and your partner approach and they engage the target by saying, *"Hi, I'm John, what's your name?"* Your target then responds, and you know their name. "Sorry, he *(points to you)* never remembers to introduce me." Everyone has a laugh, and now we all know each other's names.

To avoid awkwardness, it is important to try and commit the other person's name to memory right away. It may only last the night or the duration of the conversation, but it is important. If you care enough to learn their name, then that shows the person that you are engaged in the conversation.

If you have trouble introducing yourself, then you probably find introducing two other people to be just as tricky. This is a simple process, but it can often be complicated by nervousness. Over the course of the last ten years of marriage, I have obviously introduced my husband to many people. Often, for reasons I did not fully understand at the time, I would be quite scared to introduce him to anyone. These people ranged from strangers to dear friends; it was all the same. I was nervous every time. Finally, I came up with a rather simple trick to get over this fear, which I coined the *"Band-Aid method."*

You need to accept that the introduction of people is one social situation that you have to deal with before the conversation can truly begin. You need to take a quick breath and just do it. Pull that band-aid off, fast and hard. Don't overthink it. Removing a band-aid is not a complicated process. It requires minimal thought, and this is what I recommend for the introductions. Remember, when introducing yourself, you do **not** have to come off with something ultra-smart or witty. This is what held me back for years. My own negative voice in my head would tell me I was boring. It would tell me that I had to try and be funny or say something incredibly interesting about the other person, otherwise, everyone would think I was boring or stupid. I learned to mute the voice, and so you must do too. This same technique can be used for many other social situations, for the smaller moments.

Take a short breath and rip off the band-aid. Keep it simple.

"Jessica, this is Robin, Robin meet Jessica."

Really, that is all you need to do. I was amazed when I started to do this. How easy it could be. How I really didn't have to be this amazing entertainer just to introduce people. Rip the band-aid off!

Journaling Cue: Think of an embarrassing incident that occurred with an introduction. How did it make you feel? What could you have done differently? Do you think you may have over-thought the whole situation which leads to anxiety which in turn lead to a poor or awkward introduction?

Tips For Dealing With Other People
In my past, I would spend days beating myself up over social miscues or what I deemed to be disastrous social situations. I would play them on a loop in my head for days, and even years after. Journaling proved to be a great way to finally put some of these things behind me. I have come to realize that most of us learn more about a situation after writing it down once than they could by letting it play in their head for years. Get it down on paper and extract the lessons out of it. You may be shocked by what you discover.

Friends, family, and business associates, these groups all have different expectations of how you will behave in front of them. You don't swear in front of grandma. You don't mention your College days among your work friends. It is hard to know how to play it when these worlds collide. You don't want to offend either party.

A good rule of thumb is to raise the level of decorum to match the highest level of formality present in the group. If you are having a drink with a friend and your boss shows up, you greet him with, "Hello, sir," instead of the less formal, "Waazzzzzzup!" Maintain the formal tone with your friends until your boss has walked off, or joined another party.

Further Into Small talk

How do you make small talk? Do you feel this is one area you struggle? Small talk used to be very hard for me. For a long time, it was something that did not come naturally. It was something I actively dreaded at times, and I know I am not alone here. I have dealt with people all around the world who have said small-talk would be in their top fears.

Once you realize something, it makes it so much easier. To repeat: When it comes to small talk, it really does not matter what you talk about too much. Really. You don't have to be incredibly witty or charming. You don't have to have a world-defining point of view. Small talk is not about having a deep and meaningful conversation. Small talk is about getting comfortable and making the other person feel comfortable. That is why the weather is such a frequent topic of small talk conversation. No one can dispute weather, it is cold outside, or it is hot outside. You're not going to start a fight over the weather.

When you are engaged in small talk, keep the topics light. The rule I always adhere to is this; if you are passionate about, do **not** talk about it! Remember I am discussing small talk here which would be a situation like in a queue in a coffee shop or an elevator. When you're still in the small talk phase, people aren't ready for passion. Conversation is like starting a car on a snowy day. You need to give the car ten minutes to warm-up before you proceed up a steep hill. And you need to engage in some light small talk before you start espousing your views on the President or religion. It is a social courtesy.

Small talk is something a lot of people have difficulty with. The best advice I can give is to be prepared. The newspaper, a good quality website or even talk radio will give you good sources of topics that you can bring up. They will arm you with knowledge in areas that other people may raise. The more you know, the more confident you will be.

Questions are a safe and effective way to get a conversation going or to reignite a flagging chat. After listening to other people, you can ask questions to keep the conversation going. But, as previously covered, you need to engage in active listening. Do not spend the whole time thinking of questions to ask them back. People can see this. The danger with asking questions is that you are forcing too much of the conversational workload onto the other person. You have to remember that many other people are also uncomfortable in social situations. Many would rather listen than talk.

Remember, the goal of small-talk is to find common ground. This is the first step toward building a more meaningful relationship.

<u>Journaling Cue:</u> Why are you afraid of small talk?

Think about your experiences trying to make small talk. What is it that trips you up? Do you feel you may have been overly harsh on yourself?

Overcoming Fear

Small talk is important. Being more confident in this art will ensure you make a great first impression. However, fear is the one factor that could trip you up.

Remember this one piece of advice, if you remember nothing else from this chapter: being bad at small talk can even be the topic of small talk!

Everyone hates making small talk. I have kept conversations going by saying, *"I am sorry, I'm just terrible at small talk."* It is that simple! Generally speaking, the person that you are talking to will respond with, *"Me too,"* or *"Yeah, it's the worst."*

The conversation can build from there. You have just established common ground, and from there you can move forward.

Conversation can be complicated, but you have to remember that the other person, no matter what you may think, could be just as nervous as you.

Do Your Homework & Remember To Listen!

Anxiety is often the fear of the unknown. The more you know, the easier it can be to manage your anxiety and nerves. It is important to remember that you are trying to deal with your fear of making small talk. One of the ways to ease your anxiety is to feel prepared. You can only control the things that you can control.

I read the paper, and I check websites. It is easier to make small talk when you know what's going on in the world. As I previously said, questions can be a great way to get a conversation going. However, if you are not able to find common ground, it is impossible to move forward. That is why I always encourage people to take an interest in the world around them. The more you know, the easier it is to find common ground. I am not saying that everyone needs to be a super genius to have a conversation. Conversation is within the grasp of people of all intelligence levels. It is simply easier when you open your eyes and pay attention to the world around you.

If you feel like you are bad at small talk, it is likely because you're not listening. You're too busy waiting for your turn to talk. You are not present in the moment.

Listening to the other person is an important step if you want the small talk to transition from meaningless chatter to a deep and meaningful conversation. Deep and meaningful conversations are often the basis of establishing a friendship, relationship or valuable connection.

What Comes After Small Talk?

Once you get past the small talk, then you can have deep and meaningful conversations and build long-lasting personal relationships, should you choose.

Many people have studied long-term relationships and the benefits of them on people's lives. Few have studied the *disadvantages* of close interpersonal relationships. In his article, *"We Always Hurt the Ones We Love,"* Rowland S. Miller states, *"Many of us are routinely less courteous and tactful with our spouses than we are with most others."* He goes on to say that, *"I think that we should expect close relationships to develop a seamy underbelly over time."* Miller's article talks about the breakdown of decorum and how this leads to people abusing and mistreating the ones they love.

This breakdown in decorum is one of the reasons small talk is so important. As we allow the rules of politeness to slip away, we hurt those relationships that we have worked so hard to build. I'm not saying that the occasional lapse shouldn't be expected, but if you continue to use the art of conversation effectively, then you can maintain those relationships longer and stay close to the ones that you love.

Miller is talking specifically about spouses, but he says that his findings can be applied to all close personal relationships. The closer we get to people, the less pressure we feel to conform to the rules of polite social interaction. This is a good feeling. The conversations with your partner should be very different from those you're having with complete strangers, or your bank manager. They should be personal and intimate. However, that doesn't mean that you can throw the rules of conversing right out the window.

My favorite part of the Miller article is that he feels his findings are actually very positive. He believes that having the knowledge that your relationship is going to decay is an important tool in helping you deal with it. He believes that staying realistic with your expectations will make the decay manageable. I agree with him to an extent, although I would add that you need to do something about it before it goes too far.

The relationships that matter most to you are likely to be with spouses, friends, and family members. You need to make sure that you show them that they matter most to you. Talk to them, **actively** listen to them, and constantly try to renew and refresh the connections that made you close in the first place. We all must accept that sometimes situations and people change, this is natural. However, if the relationships are important to you, you will make an effort to maintain and in some cases rejuvenate those connections.

Small talk is a great way to start renewing those connections. I know it seems like old advice, but asking about someone's day goes a long way in showing them that you still care.

"But I ask about my partners day all the time!" I hear you say!

Ok, but take a minute to think about this and be honest with your reply. Are you really giving your partner your undivided attention? Or are you looking at your phone, watching TV, washing dishes or finishing up some paperwork? I actually caught myself in this trap only last week. I asked my husband how he was doing, but at the same time I was working on my laptop, and therefore I wasn't really paying much attention. Unbeknownst to me, he had started to talk about a colleagues Father passing away and how upsetting it was. Not giving her my proper attention I just said *"that is very sad"* and kept typing. My husband was clearly annoyed about what had happened and my lack of attention to the situation.

I put the laptop down, turned to him, and apologized. I explained that deadlines had me a bit distracted, but that was not a great excuse. We talked about it properly and maturely. This is an important part of maintaining our relationship. These conversations don't take very long to get deep and meaningful. The small talk is not nearly as long when you are talking to a spouse or close friend, but it is still important.

Giving and Receiving Complements

"I think you need to love giving compliments as much as you love receiving them."
Yami Gautam

Giving and receiving compliments sounds easy, but it is actually something that a lot of us are very poor at doing. However, with a few basic tips and tactics, it can all become a lot easier. For a long time, I had great difficulty in receiving compliments. I found it a lot easier to actually *give* them. When I was given a compliment by someone else I always, without fail, seemed to say or do the wrong thing. I was told that I would come across as either dismissive, arrogant, rude or embarrassed. I never seemed to know how to react!

In my studies and chats with people, I have found the giving and receiving of compliments to be something which trips many people up, therefore I felt it deserved its own section.

If given and received correctly, complements can be a wonderful way to make yourself and the other person feel good. It can bring people together and strengthen bonds. If done incorrectly or without confidence, then it can be a conversation killer. It can lead to possible hurt and resentment. This is as true with someone you have just met, as it is with someone you are incredibly close to, such as your spouse.

Receiving Compliments

Receiving compliments sounds like it should be the easier one, right? The reality is receiving compliments, and more accurately how you respond to the compliments, can feel a little bit like crossing a minefield! It is so easy to say the wrong thing in this situation and end up really hurting someone's feelings. It can feel simple to receive a compliment and reply with, *"Thank you,"* and feel that you have done enough. The problem is, some people are expecting that you are going to say something nice about them in return. It can be a tricky and confusing road to navigate!

Several years ago, I received my Master's degree. I had the cap, the gown, and all the usual regalia. In my mind, the day was all about me. I received a ton of compliments and congratulations from everyone who attended. I also spent quite some time congratulating many of the same people. I went through the day thinking that everyone was happy, but I came to find out, in researching this book, that many of the people I was talking to that day thought that I was coming off as smug and self-involved.

I was not paying attention to body language. I was not reading how people were receiving what I was saying. I was focused on my own accomplishments that day and while I had a right to do that, I went about it the wrong way. There is a way to enjoy your own accomplishments and still take into consideration the feelings of others. Your ungraciousness is usually due to generally feeling uncomfortable.

The worst part is that we already know the right words to say as we were taught them from a very young age. When someone says *"Thank you,"* we respond with *"You're welcome."* Literarily, it is that simple and at the same time so difficult. In the past, I would start to turn red immediately. My husband actually snuck a picture of me one time while I was receiving a compliment and it looked like I was on a rollercoaster! So how do we master the **'You're welcome?'**

Putting your needs ahead of others is the textbook definition of self-serving. It doesn't come off as humble. If you want to look humble then try waiting for them to finish and then offering them their *"You're welcome."*

The main thing is to maintain awareness in social situations. Empathy is not something that comes naturally to me. It is something I have had to work at. I had been a very self-involved person for most of my life. It took me to begin taking an active interest in what other people are doing before I started to come out of myself. My social experiences got so much better as soon as I became less concerned about myself all the time.

You don't think of yourself as selfish, or self-involved. You're just shy. However, this shyness can be interpreted by *others* as selfish and snobbish. I'm not calling you a bad person. I was not a bad person, and you aren't either. I just want you to be able to take a hard look at yourself. When you do, I also want you to realize that no matter what you see, you are still a good person! There are many things you can do to open yourself up and receive the love that the world is trying to offer you. As soon as I start throwing words around *like "self-serving"* around, people see it as a judgment. Most humans are self-serving at least to a certain degree. Maybe now is the time in your life to become more aware.

<u>Journaling Cue:</u> Why do you struggle with accepting compliments?

Think about the last time someone paid you a compliment.

Did you shut them down? Did you think of this as just you being humble?
Did you feel embarrassed or unworthy about it?
Did you struggle to know what to say?
Did you suddenly feel physically uncomfortable?

Think about the times that you have been shut down, or dismissed when you have tried to offer people compliments. How did this differ from the times when you got the *"You're welcome" response?*

Chartered Psychologist, Dr. Gary Wood tells us to think of each bit of praise as a gift. It's a great way to think about this particular problem. You wouldn't block someone from giving you a gift, would you? You wouldn't tell them that it was nothing, or try to claim that they were wrong to offer it to you. You would accept it, open it and then follow the social protocol.

You deserve praise. People are paying you a compliment because you **deserve it.** You are worthy of praise, and for people who are naturally shy, that is something we sometimes have a hard time with.

Giving Compliments

It is harder to give a compliment than most people think. So many of our compliments come off as disingenuous. You have to ask yourself, why you are giving the compliment? If the answer is, *"To get a compliment back,"* you are doing it for the wrong reason. Fishing for compliments is a phony move, and people often see right through it.

When looking at the reasons behind giving compliments, many researchers have turned to the *Social Exchange Theory*, explained here by A. Schuster.

"This theory says that people try to predict the outcome of an interaction before it takes place, and compliments and the motivation behind them can decide that outcome."

What he is saying is, this theory assumes that people are driven to act based on what they feel will benefit them the most. So for instance, they pay someone a compliment because they think that it will make that person like them – and in return, they get a compliment back.

I am not saying that these people are lying. They might really believe what they are saying, but they often have ulterior motivations behind their actions.

I believe that a compliment, to be a true compliment, needs to come from a place of sincerity. It needs to be free of self-serving motives and given without an expectation of return. There is a good chance, whenever you compliment someone, you will get **nothing** in return. You have to give the compliment fully accepting that this is the case. I know it's harder said than done, but it is something that comes easier with practice.

Compliments can be a great way to strengthen a social bond. The relationship with everyone from a romantic partner to a co-worker can grow stronger through offering a compliment. This can be a good motive, but it can also lead to hurt feelings when the compliment is not returned. Being aware of the motives behind what you said will help you to process these social encounters that do not offer the desired results.

The basis of compliments, generally speaking, differs by gender. Studies show that women are more likely to be complimented about their appearance, while men are more likely to be complimented on their skills, or a materialistic possession. An easy way to sound genuine is to be different. Don't be afraid to compliment a woman on her skills over her looks. Conversely, don't be afraid to compliment a man on his appearance.

A Quick Exercise!
This is a simple but very effective exercise that will help to reinforce the points we have just covered. The task I am setting you is to start a conversation with a compliment. My only stipulation is that it must be with a stranger. Someone you don't know at all. I know this may make it a little more difficult and might even cause some anxiety for you, but we must challenge ourselves sometimes.

Giving a compliment can be a terrific way to ease into a conversation. With a little practice, this can be a very effective tool in your social repertoire. There is nothing elaborate about this exercise; it is just good old-fashioned practice. The more you do something, the better you get.

I would encourage you to do this exercise in public spaces. Good places would be the mall, the grocery store, a social function like a wedding, or a charity event. Places where there are lots of people around.

How To Be Slightly Different!
Being generic is safe, which is why a lot of people do it. Unfortunately, the downside is that it's a good way to have your comments get lost in the sea of praise that is being offered to an individual on any given day.

It all comes back to that age-old advice again; **Don't be afraid**. I know it may seem easy for me to say, but do remember there was a time in my life when everything I am advising in this book was *incredibly* difficult for me. Do not be afraid to give out a compliment and don't be afraid to crack through the top layer and go a little deeper.

Instead of saying to someone "I like your jacket", you could say "I like your jacket – may I ask where you got it from? Seems perfect for this weather!"

Again, you do not have to go too deep, but just expanding your compliment slightly can lead to a more rewarding conversation.

Witty Banter – It Is Easier Than You Think!

"People who can't be witty exert themselves to be devout and affectionate."
George Eliot

Some people have the desire be the life and soul of the party. Others are happy just to ***attend*** the party, have some nice conversations and leave feeling relaxed and satisfied with the night's proceedings. Both sets of people have something in common here; in slightly different ways, we all want to be the guy or girl who can hold everyone's attention with their witty banter, and their clever, interesting stories. I am not going to tell you that you can't be that person. I am going to tell you to slow down.

Despite what many (*very expensive*) courses will tell you, witty banter is **not** an essential part of being a good conversationalist. You don't have to be the smartest person in the room to be someone that people want to talk to. In fact, many people are intimidated by over-the-top "clever" banter.

Once a person feels like you are talking down to them, it is very hard to keep a conversation going. Many will even respond with anger and aggression. You are making them uncomfortable.

Big words are one of the easiest ways to set people off. It is time to put away the thesaurus and just speak in a very plain, matter-of-fact way. This doesn't mean talking down to people, but you need to allow them to feel like you are having a conversation with them, not over their head.

Journaling Cue: Are you using your vocabulary to avoid people?

There are many things we do to shut other people down. Using big words is one way to tell people that you're not interested in talking to them, or that you think you're better than them. Why do you use the words that you use?

There is a time and a place for *"large words"* such as speaking at a University or taking part in a class discussion. Or if you are sitting around with a group of friends and everyone there is comfortable with this level of conversation.

This is as much about knowing your audience as it is about knowing your own limitations as a speaker. In most situations, the simplest way is the best way. Get your point across in as few words as possible.

I used to think that conversations would be easier if I could script them beforehand. I found myself walking away from a conversation and immediately the exact wording I should've used occurred to me right away! I would then kick myself for not thinking of it earlier, but the truth is that most of these *'genius things'* we think of afterward are not as perfect to others as they are to you.

This brings us to an important thing to remember when speaking about *witty banter*. What some people call funny, others call offensive. It is extremely important to be aware of this. Your jokes and clever turn of phrase may not appeal to everyone. Everyone has a different style. Everyone has a different sense of humor. You should tread lightly when going for the laugh in everyday conversation unless you know the other people very well. People would rather talk with someone who is trying to be genuine than someone who is trying too hard to be witty.

I have wasted a lot of time in my life beating myself up for not saying the right thing. I have had conversational missteps which have kept me awake at night. I would hear them in my head over and over again as I obsess over what I should have said, or how I could have sounded cooler.

As the author Judy Apps once stated, *"The art of conversation is not the same as the art of talking. Wit, eloquence and knowledge are one thing. Conversational skill is something more."* Apps describes conversation as a dance. A back and forth. At times someone has to lead, but for a dance to be successful, both partners must play a role.

A conversation is **not** a competition. A conversation is about connecting with another person. Trying to outdo the other person in a battle of wits is not going to help you build a connection. You have to ask yourself; *Is my witty banter throwing up a wall?*

I had never felt as socially isolated as I did while I was doing my Master's degree. I walked onto the University campus and tried to fit in by showing everyone my intelligence. I know now that I was spending too much time talking, and not enough time listening. However, the problem didn't end there. It was also the way I was talking to people. I was competing. I was always trying to sound smarter than everyone around me, and putting up walls in the process.

My problem was not about the words I was using. These people were all intelligent. They were very well read and articulate. The problem was the attitude I was bringing to the conversation. I desperately wanted to be the smartest person, and so I was not allowing the other people to play their part in the conversation. I was having a **monologue**, where I should have been having a **dialogue**.

The key with wit is to watch for the cues from the other person. Do they seem lost, or bored? Do they seem annoyed? There are times when wit comes off as arrogance. Use the cues, and you will be able to find the appropriate place for your witty banter.

Things to Remember
- Don't try to make others feel small.
- Realise the limits of others conversational skill.
- Have fun with language but do not go out of your way to be hilarious.
- If you feel you are not a naturally funny person, do not try too hard!
- Banter, is the same as conversation – it is a back and forth. It is not all down to you, nor is it down to the other person.
- Relax. You need to be yourself. You cannot fake this. People will see through it.

- Do not put so much pressure on yourself – NOBODY is hilarious and fascinating all the time!

How To Handle Formal Occasions

By now your knowledge and confidence about factors such as how to make small talk and how to give and receive compliments should have increased massively. Your conversation skills will be more refined. You should be starting to feel like you are better equipped to handle different situations.

Next, we need to discuss more formal settings. Unless you live like a hermit, the chances are that at least once a year you will attend a formal occasion. These events often cause a lot of anxiety in people, and it is easy to see why. Weddings, funerals, and other parties have their own rules, and you need to know them, or you will feel like a fish out of water.

As a person who used to suffer from elements of social anxiety, I know the pressure that you may feel whenever things get formal. There is just something about these milestone events that get to us. Whenever you add a dress code, you up the ante. Being invited to an event such as a wedding can seem like a dangerous proposition, but this should not stop you from enjoying how much fun and how fulfilling it can be.

I was once invited to a Sikh wedding. I had grown up with the bride, and I also knew the groom fairly well. She was not Sikh, but the parents of the groom were insistent on a traditional Sikh wedding. I have to admit I was really nervous. As the event grew ever closer, I became convinced that I was going to say or do something culturally insensitive. Not on purpose of course, but I was sure that I would stumble into causing someone offense somehow.

Thankfully my friend was very understanding about this. She had known me long enough to understand my occasional nervousness around situations like this. After talking with her about what would help me relax, she agreed to show me some basic dance steps alongside small things I should not do or say. Basically, I was given a list of actions that could cause offence! We talked about the actual wedding ritual for almost an hour.

I also did a little bit of my own prep work before the big day arrived. On the morning of the wedding, I was still more than a little apprehensive but I, of course, wanted to go for my friend. On the way to the wedding, I thought about it all more and soon realized, as I had done for other situations in the past, that nobody was there for *me*. The preparation had given me the knowledge needed to avoid offending anyone. So, with that covered, nobody would really care what I said and did. A wedding is about the bride and the groom. These are the only two people that anyone cares about watching during the wedding. Not me. Once again I had to get out of my own head and realize the world was not about me and my fears. With that realization, I had a great day out. Everything turned out to be fine, which I put down to the preparation I had done.

Journaling Cue: Is there a ceremony or event from your past that you felt went wrong?

In the past, I tended to play my mistakes over and over again in my head. Learning to write them down, briefly analyze them and then ultimately move past them was something that became easier and easier every time I did it. Now it is time to let go of one of your experiences. Something you regret. Maybe you felt you said or did the wrong thing? Maybe you felt embarrassed about something, that in reality was probably nowhere near as bad as you thought? It is time to think about it. Write down your true, honest thoughts and feelings. Briefly, analyze them.

And then, let them go.

Dealing With Sombre Occasions

I want to briefly discuss funerals. Not exactly the most light hearted topic, I know, but important. Everyone alive will someday die.

Funerals are pretty much impossible to avoid. You will have to be there for friends and relatives, time after time. It is difficult to know what to say. The basic rule when talking to anyone at a funeral is that less is more. Unless you are giving the eulogy, you should be spending less time talking and more time listening at a funeral. There is nothing you can say that is really going to help the grieving family.

"I don't know what to say," are the words you will hear all the time at funerals. It makes sense that so many people are at a loss for words. You don't want to just repeat the same things that everyone else is saying. You want to say something special, and offer some piece of advice that will make everyone feel a little better.

Unfortunately, despite your good intentions, this is practically impossible. Your wish to say something profound is a lovely thing, and it is coming from a good place, but strangely it is actually a borderline selfish thought. You have already done the most important thing; you took the time out of your day to go to the funeral. With your presence, you are showing that you care about the person. That is the most important thing.

It's not only the family that you run into at a funeral. If you are attending the funeral of an old friend, it is likely that you are going to see many people you haven't seen in a long time. This is a time for decorum. The conversation has to stay muted and respectful. A funeral is a good time to make a plan to meet later. A funeral is a great time to quietly reminisce with old friends, but if you want to reconnect this may not be the right place.

Keep it simple. Nobody expects an Oscar-winning speech to the family of the deceased. Be present, offer your condolences and leave them be unless they want to talk more.

Event Rituals
Whether it is a grade eight graduation or a bar mitzvah, every ceremony has its rituals. Do your homework. Read up on the

protocols, dress codes, and other nuances of the ceremony. Don't be afraid to ask questions. Carefully read the invitation or ticket associated with the event as in many cases there is information you need printed right there.

The biggest thing to remember is most of the time you are there for someone else. Make the day about the person you came to celebrate. This will take the pressure off of you, and allow you to enjoy yourself.

"But I'm the bride!" I hear you shout!

Oh, well, then the focus is going to be on you! You need to remember that these people are there because they love you. They didn't come to your wedding to tear you apart. They came to celebrate your big day with you.

If you are an introverted person, then you may feel like you struggle when the day is all about you. So how do you enjoy your own wedding or birthday party? Well, for starters, keep the guest list small. You want family, and close friends, people you feel comfortable around. It is completely unnecessary to have a huge guest-list, filled up with people you barely see or have any real connection with. You don't need a lot of people to have a good time. This can be hard to explain to some people, especially since larger weddings are increasingly the norm these days. If you choose a smaller venue or a destination wedding, this can usually take care of the problem for you.

As for the location, I recommend you find a safe space. Make a plan before the party starts. Find a place that is out of the way, a place you can go to recharge your batteries. When you start to feel like it's all becoming too much, disappear. Take a few minutes. Breathe. Be present in the moment. Introverted people need time out sometimes. They need to recharge alone, in a quiet place.

Dealing With A Dinner Party

You sit down at the table, and there are fifteen different utensils, three plates and a bowl filled with water. The panic begins to rise inside you. What am I supposed to do with all of *these*? Luckily, there are not many people who really understand what is going on at a fancy dinner party anymore. It is a lost art. Most people, even at weddings, are opting for less formal alternatives.

If you do find yourself face to face with a salad fork (although you may not even be a hundred percent sure that it is a salad fork), then do not be afraid to ask for help. I know that you don't want to appear foolish or uncultured, so ask one of the waiters. They had to set the table, they learned all about it, and generally speaking, they are eager to help out guests who are struggling. Oh, and it you do use this method, be sure to tip your waiter for their assistance!

Dealing with Difficult People

This is a relatively short chapter that is essentially an expansion on the classic bumper sticker, *"Mean people suck"*. This true statement should also be followed up with *"And they are everywhere."*

Mean and difficult people are unfortunately a fact of life. No matter what we do in life, there will be times when we have to deal with someone who just appears to want to be problematic, often for no good reason at all.

But despite what we think, often there is a reason. Life is not a movie; you don't always get the time to see the backstory. Usually, when someone blows up at a complete stranger or is cold and distant, there is a reason. You don't know what that person is going through. They may have lost their job, or a loved one, and not know how to deal with the stresses of their life. So when this person comes into your life and drops an anger bomb in your lap, it is important to remember that you're often not getting the whole story.

Here are a few steps that I have found helpful when dealing with difficult people.

Stay Calm
I realize that this is harder than it sounds, but if you can manage it, staying calm can be a real asset. Yelling back at a person who is shouting is only going to amp them up even more. Take a few seconds, breathe and then realize that shouting more is only going to make it worse.

Avoid Aggressive Posture
Don't confuse this with not standing your ground. If you feel the need, then stand tall and don't back away. Do not be afraid to convey confidence in these situations. However, crossing your arms, leaning in, or trying to walk closer can be seen as intimidating. Once again, the difficult person is going to increase their own aggression in response.

Try To Relate To The Aggressor…But Don't Say 'I understand'
Nothing seems to anger upset people more than people saying *'I understand.'* The thing is, in the majority of situations, you *don't* understand. Generally speaking, people aren't even yelling about what they're really upset about. Dealing with an irate person is one time where listening is definitely more about subtext than what is actually being said.

Sorry
Perhaps the most useful word in the English language, yet something many people struggle to say. Studies show that introverted people find it much easier to say sorry than extroverted people. Do not confuse saying sorry, with backing down or being weak. Usually, you say sorry when you've done something wrong. You may see it as an admission of guilt, but in this case, it is just about getting the other person to calm down. Saying sorry, and asking what you can do to help the person in question, can ease tensions, which is the goal.

Find A Solution
Try to resolve the situation with the simplest solution. This may seem like a very open-ended piece of advice, but most of the time if you can find a constructive way for them to deal with the problem, it will immediately diffuse the situation. When someone yells at you (even if the problem they are yelling about is not really the issue), they are looking for a reaction. They are looking to be appeased somehow. Diffuse the situation however you can and move on. Life is too short for a fight.

These steps are just meant to be helpful tips. Dealing with an irate person is never easy. They hold churned up emotions. Therefore it is hard to say with any certainty how they will react in any given situation. The most important thing is to stay calm and remember that this reaction is usually not your fault.

I will add one more step to the list; talk it out. One of the most effective ways to get over an incident like this is to talk through your feelings in a safe environment. Friends, family, and coworkers can provide a great sounding board to allow you to release the pent-up negative energy that builds up after you deal with a negative person.

Journaling Cue: Write it out.

Take a few minutes and think about an encounter in your past with a difficult person.

What was your role in their freak out?
What did you do to deal with the situation?
Try to take your mind back to that time. Visualize the situation as best as you can.
What were you thinking?
What were you feeling?
What did you do?

Dealing with irate people is hard for anyone. It is tough to remain calm when people are losing their heads. Make sure that you give yourself a pat on the back for making it through this ordeal. Even if you don't make it through completely unscathed, realize that it is a tough situation and at least you tried.

One last point to repeat is this; try not to judge the difficult person. Earlier in the book we talked about your inner voice; that voice that judges you in your head as you walk around and try to go about your day. Judging other people is like food for this inner voice. The more judgemental you are of others, the more judgemental they will be with you, and this can lead to problems with social interactions.

In my past, I know that I missed out on several opportunities for fear of looking silly. This all comes from being too judgemental. I know what I think about people when they make a mistake or lose their temper. I would never want other people to think about me like that. Our judgemental nature can hold us back.

This is why it is so important to talk after a situation like this. When you talk through your feelings, you can also resolve any of the judgments that you may have developed for the person. You can decide that you likely just caught them at a bad time, or that something else had to be going on. By consciously going through this process you can undo some of the damage that the incident has caused in terms of adding to your judgemental nature.

Moving On With Life

Journaling Cue: What have you learned?

Take a few minutes and reflect on what you have learned in this book. Make a plan for continuing this journey. You have learned the techniques, and now you need to get out there and practice them; get out there and talk to people!

Hopefully, by now, you realize you don't have to be the life and soul of the party. You don't have to run into a room, do a backward somersault and tell a hilarious joke. You can be quiet. You can be yourself. But do not deny yourself of social interactions. They can bring so much light, love, and joy to life.

Be aware of your physical self. Your body is saying as much to other people as your words are, if not more. Be aware of the messages your posture and eyes are sending out to people. Be present and be aware. Once you understand the message that you are sending out to people, then you can adjust accordingly.

It's like being your own PR agency. You need to find your own brand, and then tailor it to find how to best present yourself to people. Think about celebrities and the teams that they employ just to work on their image; agents, PR guys, aestheticians, and the whole entourage. I don't know about you, but I can't afford that kind of help. So we have to do this for ourselves!

Don't believe what some people tell you. Apart from a very few select life situations, hard and fast rules don't really exist in social interactions. I used to secretly wish that I could be the writer in my life. Conversations would be so easy if I could just control what everyone else was saying. I would hand everyone their lines at the beginning of the day, and they would go about their lives, sticking to the script, no surprises, no shocks, never being caught off guard. But what sort of life would that actually be? Life is about changes. It is fluid. It is not scripted, it is not stale.

In the real world, you can never really know how another person is going to react. There are things that you can do to increase your chances of a favorable response, but there are no guarantees. There is no perfect amount of eye contact that works for every person in every conversation. There is no perfect phrase that will suddenly overnight make everyone an incredible conversationalist. Life does not work like that. People aren't perfect, and life isn't perfect. Accept this and roll with the punches.

In a world where anything can happen, and perfection is impossible, we have the freedom to get out there and make mistakes. We don't have to spend all our time worrying about getting things right on the first try. We don't have to walk around fretting about saying something wrong because, well, the fretting will not change much. We will all sometimes say the wrong thing. We are human.

The best advice I can give you for making mistakes is to **own them**. The very action of taking responsibility for your mistakes and owning your faults can be a very freeing thing. If you feel you have said or done the wrong thing, give a humble, open and honest apology. The mistakes in my life that I truly regret are the ones that I didn't take ownership of. I regret the ones I lied about and the ones I tried to cover up. But I have never regretted the mistakes that I truly accepted responsibility for and apologized for. When you apologize for a mistake, you have taken the first vital step towards putting it behind you. This will be part of a process that makes you a better and more sincere conversationalist in the future. You will feel better about yourself. You will stand taller, look people in the eye, and you will speak without fear of mistakes.

Fear is one of the biggest obstacles to meaningful conversation. A fear of opening up, a fear of meeting new people, a fear of being judged, a fear of looking silly, the list goes on. The only way to deal with the fear is to desensitize yourself. You do this through consistent practice. I have lost many nights of sleep dealing with my issues about conversations, introversion, shyness and social anxiety. I would stare up at the ceiling and think about the people I was going to have to talk to in the morning. I would imagine things going wrong. I would think about the presentation that I had to give. The worrying accomplished nothing. It was unproductive and unhelpful.

Fear is natural and it will never fully go away. This is something you need to accept, but you also have to understand that is a good thing. As I have already said in this book, a little fear keeps you on your toes. It also helps you to remember the rules of conversing. If you get too comfortable, you will fall back into bad habits. Embrace the fear and use it to make you a better speaker, and a better listener.

There was a time that I avoided many social situations. When I had to be around people, I fretted about what I would say. I constantly worried about saying the wrong thing. I would lie in bed at night and play over and over any conversations I had had that day. I would convince myself I had done wrong and everyone was either laughing at me or just thought I was stupid.

Using the advice in this book, I slowly became better. I learned to relax. I now speak at conferences around the world and can mingle around a party with ease. I am still an introverted person, and I am happy with that. I will never be the loud, outgoing party girl. I don't even want to be. I want to be **me**.

Life is about people. The connections, the conversations and the moments we remember for the rest of our lives. Do not deprive yourself of any of this. You can be anyone you want to be. Believe in yourself, embrace the world…and have fun. I wish you all the luck in the world. Thank you for reading.

Printed in Poland
by Amazon Fulfillment
Poland Sp. z o.o., Wrocław